¡Gila Libre!

¡Gila Libre!

NEW MEXICO'S
LAST WILD RIVER

M. H. Dutch Salmon

M. H. SALMON

UNIVERSITY OF NEW MEXICO PRESS ◆ ALBUQUERQUE

13 12 11 10 09 08   1 2 3 4 5 6

LIBRARY OF CONGRESS CATALOGING-IN-PUBLICATION DATA
Salmon, M. H., 1945–
Gila libre! : New Mexico's last wild river / M.H. Salmon.
p. cm.
ISBN 978-0-8263-4082-5 (PBK. : ALK. PAPER)
1. Gila River (N.M. and Ariz.)—History.
2. Gila River Region (N.M. and Ariz.)—History.
I. Title.
F817.G52S26   2008
917.91'702—dc22

2008025272

Reproductions by Tom Steinbach from *Mimbres Classic Mysteries:
Reconstructing a Lost Culture Through Its Pottery* by
Tom Steinbach and Peter Steinbach, published by
Museum of New Mexico Press, © 2002 Tom Steinbach.
All rights reserved.

FRONTIS: Looking upstream toward defunct Hooker Dam site.
Courtesy of Jan Haley

Book design and type composition by Kathleen Sparkes.
This book was designed using Minion OT PRO 11/14, 26P.
Display is Brioso OT PRO and Minion OT PRO.

☾

Dedicated to the upper Gila watershed,

a natural world that so many of the well intended

have been trying for so long to develop into something new.

May they see the light.

Contents

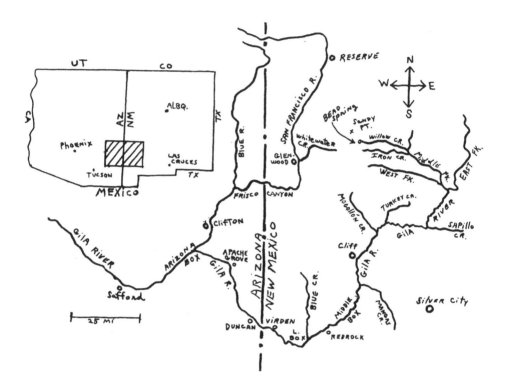

Gila Descending map. Courtesy of M. H. Salmon.

Introduction

◊

ON MY FIRST VISIT TO THE RIVER, OR AT LEAST THAT PARTICULAR section of it, I nearly turned away. I was in poor humor anyway. Risking an overworked phrase, I'll call it "female trouble." Lay no blame, but suffice it to say the lot of them had led me to seek surcease at a portion of the world that was new to me and where, I was told, a river named "Gila" offered sporting fish. But this was no river. It was a stream, and standing on the bank I could see that if you picked out a riffle, you could cross on foot without wetting your knees. Hardly even your ankles. I knew rivers—the St. Lawrence, the Seneca, the Oswego, the Salmon, the Black, the Nueces. A real river could float a freighter, or at the least a barge, a yacht, a bass or drift boat. This Gila would ground a canoe.

There were other discouragements. Unthinking, I had picked a Sunday. I arrived near midday, and with church out the revelers had beat me to it. For me "church" has always been found along the waters, but for spiritual revelations this was not the place. Under a few old and splendid sycamores the dust rose behind big tires as the ATVs and pickups circled the picnic grounds. Swimmers filled the scattered pools, no doubt outnumbering the fish in places. Young adults played grab-ass in and out of the water, and everyone seemed frantically happy. If anyone there but me was seeking the solace of running waters, it wasn't apparent. I picked up the trail that vehicles preceding me had turned into a maybeso road and started upstream.

With good management, grazing can work, even in the West and even along streams in the Southwest. But that day along the Gila it wasn't working. The occasional big and splendid sycamore, cottonwood, hackberry, box elder, and oak stood stately but scattered and largely solitary, with little ground cover or second growth to hold the banks and sustain a future. The cows munched at will at the remaining seep willows and stared vacantly at my passing. It was easy walking. The "road" had cleared the path, and where it met the stream at most every sharp bend, the terrain forced a crossing. Near these bends and crossings lay the pools. Most had already been claimed by a pickup or two, and their riders, I confess, were mostly friendlier than I; they waved a hand and said, "Any luck?" I waved my pole and shook my head.

The river disappointing, I made time along the road and raised my eyes to the vistas. They were most spectacular up ahead a mile or so, where the river made a sharp turn and narrowed between canyon walls—"The Box." No cow or ATV could climb those canyon cliffs, and no backpacker was likely to try. They looked just as nature made them—a changing array of reds and pinks and grays and blacks as the sun turned over scattered clouds and alternately lit and shaded a thousand feet of precipitous cline. I made The Box and kept going, to where the river made another sharp turn, an "S" in the canyon. Here, I'd been told, the Bureau of Reclamation had a plan to build a dam, make a lake, and pump a significant portion of the river's slim flow to the nearest urban area, some thirty miles away. This dam would fall in time to various public objections, only to be revived in recent years, some two decades later, as a diversion project with off-stream storage, which, according to its proponents, would be more environmentally benign. Back then I only knew what one local had told me: "The Hooker Dam is coming; better see the river now before it's gone."

I had hiked two miles and more and it seemed I had put the last of vehicular traffic behind me; I could still hear voices, machinery, and a boom box or two, but it seemed it was now all back downstream. I crept up to the edge of the green pool washed out deep by the current against the rock wall where the government and its boosters planned on packing all that cement. I saw several smallmouth bass, visible as cruising shadows in the depths. Smallmouth bass? What are they doing here, west of the Continental Divide? I was geared for catfish. I love catfish. And nature never put a smallmouth bass within five hundred miles of this place. But that's what I saw, and I was intrigued.

Stepping back, I dropped my pack, scooped a waterdog from out of the bait bucket, and skewered him through the base of the tail. I lofted him out and when he hit the water, he quit struggling and sank slowly, his limbs outstretched like a sky diver. He went down and out of sight and promptly something picked him up. I struck, then gave line to one wicked run, and then the hook pulled out. The waterdog had come loose too.

Next time I fished out the smallest waterdog in the bucket. I lofted him to the stream and out and down he went and just as promptly something picked him up. The fish headed for the bottom, pulled strongly, briefly, and then I lost him. I tried once more and this time put the bait in the water where I could see the approach. A nice bass came from out of the hole, shoveled up a good portion of the waterdog, but didn't get much of the hook. He ran off, I struck, and he left like the others with my bait. I thought, I have hiked two miles and more to feed a school of bass a lot smarter than I am.

These waterdogs were about right for catfish, five pounds and up, which is what I'd been fishing for all summer. They were too large for bass twelve to fifteen inches long. More to the point, they were fine for the bass, too big for the fishing.

I went upstream to the next pool, halted, and tied on a spinner. Keeping well away, I lifted the spinner on a quartering cast to the head of the pool, let it sink and drift with the flow, then drew it briskly back up-current. I hooked one, kept pressure on, but didn't horse him. My spinning rod was light, whippy, and I let the fish wear himself out. He covered the pool a half dozen times doing it. He came in slick and green with bronze highlights that blossomed in the sun. I kept him.

The good fight had spooked the rest of them. I fished a can of sardines out of my pack, leaned up against a log underneath a big sycamore, opened the can, and had supper, stabbing the little fish and eating them off my knife without greasing my hands or cutting my tongue. And the coffee in the thermos was still hot. There was more shade than sun now in the canyon, and it was pleasant and cool in the shade where I ate. Tomorrow, I thought, is a work day. Not for me, still being among the unemployed in my new surroundings, but for others in the canyon, for I heard the last crew I had passed gathering up and motoring away downstream. Then it really got quiet. I had come here for this.

Perhaps I could find home here after all? True, this stretch of river lacked a certain management ethic, but that could be fixed, and I had never anywhere seen the likes of these canyon walls. Geronimo was raised here at the headwaters of the Gila, saw the same vistas, and fought memorably to keep them. Ben Lilly, quintessential hunter, last of the mountain men, and proverbial odd duck was raised elsewhere, but in a lifetime of hunting all over chose these mountains as his place to stay, pursue bear and lion, and die of natural causes. Aldo Leopold, America's patron saint of conservation, was inspired by the headwaters of the Gila, successfully promoting this forest as our nation's first wilderness area. I had just caught the gamest fish that swims from its waters! A fisher could knock himself out here—trout in the colder waters above, catfish in the warmer waters below, and bronze bass in between, overlapping both. They all three are good, wherever you can catch them, but to catch them in a place like this! And what would it be to try these bass on flies? I imagined that I could view myself from one of the cliffs towering above, knee-deep in the stream and throwing a long loop, a small, middling angler surrounded by majesty. I sure didn't need any more female trouble, but in a place like this you can't help but think: Someday, I'd like to share all this with the right woman.

I raised my eyes to the sycamore that shaded me and slowly gathered the implications—there was heavy slash held in its branches, ten feet above. I was already well above the stream, and what torrent of water would fill this canyon wall to wall, carrying loose limbs to the treetops? Could it be the same river I fished and crossed on foot without getting my wallet wet? I'd arrived disappointed; now there was more to this Gila River than I could imagine.

Six bighorn sheep, three ewes and three lambs, came down out of the rough hills to the river about fifty yards upstream. The canyon was now so quiet, they made a clatter coming over the rocks and I heard them before I saw them. They stopped to drink, crossed over, and slowly diminished into the cliffs on the north side, going up the rocks and impossible incline with confidence and a seeming nonchalance. I watched them go for a long time. Then I fell asleep . . .

. . . Upstream in long shadows I found an oversize hellgrammite under a big rock in mud flats well away from the stream. Surely fishing with what the fish normally eats, and catching it yourself, is the most natural way to angle. He was a nasty looking beggar, nearly the size of my little finger, and mean and not happy with his prospects. His pincers had impressive strength, but I got him hooked on the end of a long leader with a small sliding sinker above the swivel. I tossed him upstream and let him drift down into the new pool. There was a quick response in the deep water; the line checked, I gave a little slack, then drew up firm and said, "Mister, you have had it!" A good bass; quick, tough, and a leaper.

Two, each a little over a foot long, were just right to take home for breakfast. And it was getting dark. Down out of The Box, nearing the truck in a long stretch of slack water, a great blue heron lifted off, nearly invisible against the darkening hills, then a clear silhouette led by an arched neck up against the backlit sky that was a little pink, a little blue, with a few wispy clouds. The last of the revelers, a quiet, sleepy-eyed boy, was drifting on down to the picnic grounds on an inner tube; he had his head tilted back in a reverie, watching that big bird, and didn't seem to notice me as I walked by.

Bead Spring. Courtesy of Jan Haley.

An Unlikely Place for Water

"IN THIS DEAD LAND, LIKE A VAST RELIEF MODEL, THE ONLY ALLEGIANCE was to sun." So wrote Walter Van Tilburg Clark in "The Indian Well," as good a short story as you will ever read. His narrative takes place in desert; it does seem dead at a glance. Moonscape. Live there, though, and the desert comes alive, much like Van Tilburg Clark's "The Indian Well," with a variety of tough, resilient inhabitants, most of them at once furtive and ironically colorful, in a place where human histories and their characters, and natural histories and their characters, mix, clash, and tell hard-bitten tales that could happen nowhere else. Clark's story emerged from a perennial spring. It all came from improbable waters bringing life to an unlikely place you wouldn't think could hold it. Such a place is southwest New Mexico.

Its *principal* allegiance is to sun—it shines about 80 percent of the time over a region a bit larger than the state of Maine. Aridity is pervasive. In the south, Deming and Lordsburg, despite more than 4,000 feet of elevation, are classic desert, receiving on average only eight inches of precipitation a year. A rule of thumb has it that more elevation yields more precipitation; five inches or more should come with every thousand feet. Yet at the northern edge of this region Quemado sits high and dry, with barely twelve inches per year at 7,000 feet. Along the eastern boundary, where the Rio Grande flows south, Socorro, Truth or Consequences, and Las Cruces are all limited by less than ten inches of rain per year; most of the year the lot of them are dry as a chip. There's hardly any habitation along the western border with Arizona, but Glenwood is centered along that line; it's surrounded by mountains and is bisected by two slim running waters. Yet the town itself misses most of the rain. Southwest of Socorro, two isolated mountain ranges, the Magdalenas and the San Mateos, feature peaks over 10,000 feet. Big trees and spectacular vistas can be found in those heights—mountain islands rising above desert seas. As on the desert below, there is life there, and hidden springs. It's not Gila monsters and Aplomado falcons, but elk, bears, and a melanistic type of tassel-eared squirrel. So these mountains are not a desert, but for all the Ponderosa pine, spruce, fir, and aspen, you won't find a trout, minnow, or a single perennial flowing stream. Taking up a full quarter of the state, but seemingly much detached from the rest of New Mexico, geographically, politically, and culturally, none of southwest New Mexico's seven counties—Doña Ana, Luna, Hidalgo, Grant, Catron, Socorro, or Sierra—holds a town with a hundred thousand people. Of course even more aridity and heat haven't held Phoenix back, but New Mexico's southwestern counties stand largely untroubled by growth. This is remarkable since the region has a verdant heartland, the Gila River headwaters, standing tall and lovely at the center and gathering all the rain and snow its surroundings consistently and sorely miss.

It's an unlikely place for water. But east of Glenwood and south of Reserve, and west of Truth or Consequences and north of Silver City, the land form suddenly defies desert and comes up quickly and steep and rough and high—the Black Range, the Pinos Altos Range, the mighty Mogollon Range; the quirk in topography jolts the weather from its arid sameness and, by golly, it rains here. Snows too.

In March 2005 the SNOTEL marker at Whitewater Baldy, the Gila's highest peak at 10,897 feet, marked the snow depth at an astonishing twelve feet, the highest reading in the state. Any of this mountainous Gila terrain approaching 9,000 feet or better will average thirty to forty inches of precipitation per year. And it's a pretty good expanse of mountains, most of it national forest, called the Gila, of course, and totaling 3.3 million acres of public land. None of this produces anything an easterner would call a river, except at flood stage, but it does produce perennial springs that feed perennial creeks that feed the perennial middle, east, and west forks of the Gila River. The San Francisco River, a tributary of the Gila that feeds in just over the Arizona line, sports a similarly slim but precious flow, while the Mimbres River, which like the east fork of the Gila comes out of the Black Range, is perennial in the forest before sinking into the sands of the Chihuahuan desert north of Deming. Together, all of these "rivers" and their tributaries total at best perhaps one thousand miles of perennial stream. Not a lot of water, and yet it's always there, it remains largely and improbably unmolested, and, considering its arid surroundings, comes as a constant and ever-pleasant surprise.

This improbably verdant uplift is rare, dear, and fecund—it gives life in remarkable and variegated forms. Nowhere else do the Rocky Mountains of northern climes blend so seamlessly with the Sierra Madre of Mexico. As the crow flies, towering Englemann spruce grow but a few miles from stands of Apache pine. On the same day you might see a red squirrel and a javelina, an elk and a coatimundi, a mule deer and a Gila monster, or a great horned owl and a Mexican black hawk. On the same day of fishing you might catch a Gila/rainbow hybrid trout and a flathead catfish. Possibly even from the same pool! A rich ecological niche, this Gila country, due in part to the unique stretch of topography that touches both northern and southern climes. But that alone would mean much less if the mountains, canyons, and desert reaches could not, like the San Mateos, maintain a perennial-flowing watershed. To be sure, there are droughts almost yearly. Each spring, April, May, and June are typically dry months, even in the high country, with aridity often aggravated by dusty winds. October and November are typically dry too. But monsoon rains in July, August, and September come in from the southwest and revive the forest and the desert below. Winters may be relatively moist as well. In lower elevations this winter precipitation is often rain, or snow that melts off in a day or two. Above 8,000 feet the snow can pile up. Twelve feet deep is not typical, but it is not uncommon for the high country around Whitewater Baldy, deep in the Gila Wilderness, to lead the state in SNOTEL depth at the peak of winter.

Follow the middle fork of the Gila River, from a source like Bead Spring at over 10,000 feet to the Arizona line at nearly 4,000 feet, and you will visit five life zones in a reach of perhaps 150 miles. Englemann and blue spruce of the Hudsonian zone yield to the Douglas fir and aspen of the Canadian zone, which in turn blend with the Ponderosa and oak of the Transition zone, which in time mix with the piñon and juniper of the upper Sonoran zone, and on down to the ocotillo, cholla, and sundry claret cactus that at least partake of traits of the lower Sonoran desert. A variegated mix of biomes, including broad grasslands where no trees or brush grow at all, all virtually holding hands in one section of public land and enlivened by the richest zone of all, the riparian zone where the waters flow—it cuts, connects, and feeds all the others, sporting cottonwood, sycamore, willows, hackberry, box elder, Emory oak, and a myriad of other plants that wouldn't be there without the water. Best of all, most of this flow is within public lands. The watershed of the three forks is within the wilderness zone; the middle and west forks each close to forty miles long; the east fork, which carries more water, about thirty miles long. The Upper Box, from where the forks join down to Mogollon Creek—some forty-two miles—is also mostly wilderness, and the elevation drops about 1,500 feet. The river then enters the Cliff/Gila Valley, an agricultural reach of some twenty miles, so far unsullied by urban sprawl. Follow the currents and there comes the Middle Box, more national forest, a deeply sliced canyon of class IV rapids and giant catfish that emerges onto the Red Rock Valley, and more scattered farms and ranches. The Lower Box below is a BLM wilderness study area, another canyon reach perhaps fifteen miles long with class I rapids. The Gila then flows through farm country for some fifty miles into Arizona to a wonderful public canyon, the Gila Box Riparian National Conservation Area, where it merges with the San Francisco River. It augments the Gila's flow, but both flows are largely diverted some dozen miles downstream and the Gila essentially ends as a natural river. It soon enters San Carlos Reservoir, sometimes full, sometimes empty, but beyond the Gila offers little as a natural phenomenon; by the time it reaches the Phoenix area it is almost always a dry wash. The historic Gila was perennial all the way, but of nearly seven hundred miles from source to the Colorado River, barely one third today retains anything of the natural world to save.

It is the upper Gila watershed that has largely escaped "development"; it is the subject of our story and is a western paradigm. The variety in the region's "western" wildlife, topography, and natural history has been alluded to. Its current human inhabitants tell a western story as well. Nobody lives in the Gila forest's 3.3 million public forest acres, yet it is commonly visited. Of the communities that surround it—those close enough to actually view the mountains—none can muster more than about ten thousand people. But all the ingredients of the Old West/ New West clash of cultures are present: ranchers and retirees; right wing rednecks and Gucci liberals; saddle shops and espresso houses; growth mongers and eco-freaks; Anglos and Hispanics; preservationists and trophy hunters; backpackers, horsepackers, and ATV noisemakers; art galleries; general and "dry goods" stores (remember them?); and, lately, Big Box-Mart. Some of these people don't really like each other much, but, with rare exceptions, they all get along.

The region's natural history largely generated, determined, and continues to influence its human history. That history is at once prototypical western, and yet extraordinary. None of the people in this narrative would have come—or at least would not have stayed—without the water. Follow their tracks and, all told, it's a remarkable trail of characters: primitive artists with talents that continue to astound the most modern critics; equine warriors who proved the last holdouts of the Indian wars; mountain men, tough, quirky, and mean; ranchers, farmers, and homesteaders, some literate and profound, others shortsighted and ignorant; seminal conservationists inspired by the region's land and waters to create a new American environmental legacy; rapacious developers inspired by other possibilities for the same resource and hard at work to see the region and its flowing waters "developed."

Recreationists have always found the Gila headwaters an attraction, though the roughness of terrain and lack of roads have always limited their number. But they came in the nineteenth century, all through the twentieth, and now in the twenty-first to pursue the game and fish, or challenge themselves with the terrain and wild waters, or commune with a still natural world.

The Gila region of New Mexico yields up typical western tales peopled by some atypical folks. The paradigm weakens, the prototype breaks down, only at the river. Unlike so many main-stem western streams, New Mexico's Gila River still flows free. So far. Thus this maybeso river is something of a western anomaly. Its denouement is not yet known.

Shaman's balance staff. From *Mimbres Classic Mysteries: Reconstructing a Lost Culture Through Its Pottery* by Tom Steinbach and Peter Steinbach. Courtesy of Museum of New Mexico Press, Santa Fe, New Mexico.

A People Lost and Found

Across the Southwest, those who came ahead of the harrier Apaches are called the "ancient ones." That's *our* appellation, not theirs, but it seems good enough to describe a culture that came in about the time of Christ, gradually developed, finally and briefly flourished, then broke up and dissolved about eight hundred years ago. And of all those ancient ones and their southwestern subcultures, none has received more study than the Mimbres group of the Mogollon culture of southwest New Mexico. This subculture was never as large, developed, or advanced as some others of the ancient ones, further north in New Mexico and further west in Arizona, but they left an amazing art, by acclamation the best of its time. How good is it?

In *Sky Determines* Ross Calvin focuses, like most critics, on the bowls holding geometric designs. He writes, "By far the finest craftsmanship is shown, so the present writer feels, in the geometric bowls. Says A. V. Kidder, 'No ware of the Southwest can approach that of the Mimbres either in technical perfection of brushwork, or in the variety, freedom and sheer boldness of its decorative conception. It is amazing stuff.'"

Elsewhere Calvin reinforces his opinion: "In *Art and Archeology* the eminent French critic Dr. Salomon Reinach was recently quoted . . . as saying that in abstract geometric design even the Greeks were inferior to the Mimbreños."

I wouldn't argue, yet I have always been most captured not by the geometric innovations, but rather by the realistic or naturalistic designs, almost always more emotive than literal, where the Mimbres depicted their natural world and human emotions, and told stories.

Indeed, they explored with their art every corner of the human dilemma, every urge, trial, need, and dream found in a human life, and left a record. It wasn't a written record, and the oral record was lost because the people disappeared. It was all to be found in a peculiar form of art, left behind on painted bowls, on rocks and cliff faces, often hidden away in caves, tombs, and crumbled dwellings. A lot was lost to time, or clumsy pothunters, but what has been found is astounding.

Of course they made their camps along the waters. Nowadays you can sink wells in the desert, far from any stream, and create a small city like Deming, or a big one like Tucson. Or, like Phoenix, you can dry up two rivers (the Salt and the Gila) and divert enough acre feet from another one (the Colorado) to sprout a million households. But the ancient ones had to look for running water. The artists in question walked in, probably from the south, from Mexico, and found those precious perennial flows along the Mimbres, Gila, and San Francisco rivers and tributaries. Even the valleys weren't flat, but patches of level land offered prospects for farming. That's where most of the game was too, along or near the waters. Pit houses yielded over time to rough structures above ground, and some people made use of caves in cliffs. Any way they hooded up from the elements, it was camping out by our standards. But for a while they did all right.

Irrigation agriculture must have been tempting. Divert a perennial flow to a ditch and then to a field and create a steady supply of water that you can turn on and off even if only with hand labor and primitive tools. These people did that, but it often would have been frustrating. All three watersheds are so volatile. There would be times when the flow got too slim and competition for water would leave some fields dry. Alternatively, floods could wipe away the crop and sometimes the field itself with its precious soil. So I'm thinking these people were also practitioners of "Indian farming."

That's what I call it and I've done it myself. In the valleys where they lived, which are foothill elevations running generally between 5,000 and 6,000 feet, tree ring data suggests rainfall averaged about fifteen inches per year—about what it does today. That's a semi-arid environment and doesn't sound like farm country. But in Gila country more

Corn planters and Mimbres farming. From *Mimbres Classic Mysteries: Reconstructing a Lost Culture Through Its Pottery* by Tom Steinbach and Peter Steinbach. Courtesy of Museum of New Mexico Press, Santa Fe, New Mexico.

than half of that precipitation falls in just three months—July, August, and September. Irrigation farmers would have planted in the spring. Attuned to the natural world in a way a modern man can never know, the Mimbres/Gila valley farmer had another option, as he could smell the coming of the monsoons. Plant a seventy-five-day corn the first week of July, catch eight inches of rain well spaced over the same number of days, and you can make a crop while the days are still long and warm and before the first frost. I don't farm like my life depends on it, so I'm not that good, but I've done it myself, this Indian farming, and made a crop more years than not in the same locale.

And the Indian farmer would go to extraordinary lengths to make food. Not so many years ago a teenaged tourist turned up two large ollas in a cave not far off the paved road. I mean *large* ollas; filled with water, it would take a very strong person to lift one. On a family-sized corn patch a farmer with nothing but labor and time—and these folks had plenty of both—could haul enough water to soak individual corn or bean plants to tide them over to the next rain. If your life depended on it, you wouldn't even call it work.

I can only speculate on the details, and it's fun to do so. But we do know they farmed and that the occupation was not only a necessity, but also well revered. For some of these farmers were artists.

Depicted on one decorated bowl, a team of corn planters seem to revel in their work, squaring out a field, lining out rows, using flattened sticks to make holes for the seeds and cultivate the grounds. These workers are all men, the phallus subtle but evident on each figure. On another bowl, naked corn maidens hold some religious significance, a hopeful link between the hard realities of farmwork and the vagaries of weather and whoever it was they prayed to, to bring them clouds, rain, and flowing streams. Other agricultural images are celebratory: workers, usually women, burdened with enormous baskets of crop are stooped by the weight, yet the animator still captured humans exalted by the satisfaction any farmer of any era knows when the yield is good and the future, at least for a time, secured.

Hunting and fishing were also important for subsistence in the Gila and Mimbres watersheds of the time. The artists tell us favored game of the hunters was deer, turkey, and hares, in our West known as jackrabbits. Hunting too is hard physical labor, especially with primitive

Deer hunters. From *Mimbres Classic Mysteries: Reconstructing a Lost Culture Through Its Pottery* by Tom Steinbach and Peter Steinbach. Courtesy of Museum of New Mexico Press, Santa Fe, New Mexico.

weapons and not even a horse for transportation. In sport hunting that we moderns are familiar with, it is possible to say that "the chase is the thing." The Mimbres also celebrated the chase, for they frequently recounted it on their bowls and rock art. The "thing," though, was to bring the game down and get their hands bloody; on the thin trail of subsistence a good hunting story back at camp wasn't worth much if there was no meat for the pot. Amazing, therefore, that the Mimbres, who doubtless often hunted while desperate for a meal, left hunting scenes filled with such charm, the game delightfully animated, sometimes with exaggerated traits, and the pursuit a religious experience, with the hunters often carrying a bow and arrow in one hand and a prayer stick in the other.

Historically the Mimbres River held no fish of size; the largest, the Chihuahuan chub, averages a mere five to eight inches. But the Gila River held the Gila trout, the desert sucker and Sonoran sucker, and the roundtail chub, any of which could reach two feet and several pounds in weight. The Mimbres fished the Gila; indeed, fish are common images in their art. One splendid bowl I've seen shows a proud fisherman with a full catch, a hero shot worthy of *Field & Stream*. The artist even went to the trouble to record the handheld seine, made of some sort of tough natural fiber, that was used to trap the fish, and showed the smaller fish strung up on a stick stringer. That's an old trick and rural kids still do it today. In a pinch, stranded in camp without a stringer, I've done it myself with Gila River catfish. The Mimbres fished out of necessity, but they brought the same charm and lively animation to the fish as to the game when it came time to tell their fish stories on bowls, rocks, and cliff faces; in one image they left behind they seem to be following fish into the afterlife.

In art, when does the erotic lean too far and grade into the pornographic? Even the Supreme Court can't tell us for sure. The Mimbres artists apparently feared no censures and they too toyed with that fine line. Some images I've seen, seldom reproduced, seem as raunchy as the stuff they paint on the men's room wall right above the urinal down at the local honky-tonk. The familiar Mimbres lothario who we call Kokopelli, with his prayer stick in one hand and his erection in the other, passes muster with most modern sensibilities. He's lusty without being crude and captures us with his candor and the twinkle in his eye. He is also

Proud fisherman. From *Mimbres Classic Mysteries: Reconstructing a Lost Culture Through Its Pottery* by Tom Steinbach and Peter Steinbach. Courtesy of Museum of New Mexico Press, Santa Fe, New Mexico.

often shown playing the flute, while leading women off to assignations only hinted at by his animated self-confidence and their apparent compliance. Men's fantasies haven't changed much over time.

A deeper and more confounding piece of erotica is the image of the poor bloke whose extended organ has got the best of him. Out of all proportion with normalcy, *it* is now controlling *him*. Some people look at this one and think it's funny, or crude, or gross. I don't think it's funny or crude or gross. Nor was it meant to be. Over the centuries, a number of great writers have written long novels about love/lust obsessions that have driven either a male or female character to the brink. One Mimbres artist captured that whole story in a simple image.

Birthing babies, child rearing, marriage, attempted communions with the spirits—it's all there, and some of it recovered and reproduced, that we might ponder what they did, thought, loved, and feared long ago. View the whole spectrum of their lives, as seen through their art, and one must conclude that in all the essentials, *they are us*. It was a creative arc that was a long time coming, and it didn't last.

The first thousand years of this Mogollon culture produced little of artistic value. Compared to the masterwork to come, these people produced pots and bowls that were plainly decorated, if at all, and functioned primarily as tools or utensils. The evidence suggests the culture was gradually flourishing, however, with expanded populations resulting from a generally favorable climate, improved technologies, and adaptations to the natural world. Then about 1000 AD, the proliferation of master art began. Many say all the artists were women. Some have said it was just one woman, or a mere handful in a very limited number of communities. My guess is that the artists were as prolific as the art, and that the remarkable innovation and creativity, which seems to have come out of nowhere, was largely the result of a certain number of talented souls finding themselves with some relative leisure time. In practical ways, the culture had advanced. Success relieved the artists for a time from pure, hardscrabble subsistence and gave them the time and inclination to create. For a century and a half, maybe two, life was particularly good. Artists, who left images for all time, among others, flourished. But it was a culture that was not sustainable.

There is some evidence of what happened to the Mimbres culture, which can lead to suppositions and hypothesis. A theory perhaps. Even

Mimbres Erotica. From *Signal to Depart: A Novel* by M. H. Salmon. Courtesy of High-Lonesome Books, Silver City, New Mexico.

amongst the best-educated, it's still a guess. I'm not among the best-educated, just a casual observer, but it's a pleasant fascination to try and put it all together.

By 1000 AD populations had flourished into the thousands up and down the Mimbres and Gila valleys. For a time their numbers continued to grow. But the very growth made life more difficult. Wood, game, fish, nuts, berries, things you need, were no longer close by as the burgeoning populations gathered them up. Success meant hunting forays further afield. A deer, a turkey, even a hare began to look like a rare prize. They had no livestock. Farming may have become a greater struggle as well. There were more mouths to feed now, and soils may have become depleted. How much did the Mimbres know about crop rotations, green manures, how to fallow ground, the perils of salinity from overuse of irrigation? In the early days, you just moved on to another field, broke new ground. But there were more people now, a lot more; there was no new ground and perhaps no art of agriculture fine enough to restore the older fields. How many farmers even today would have the knowledge to maintain soil fertility without frequent trips to the feedstore for sacks of a careful mix of nitrogen, potash, and phosphate?

Tree ring data tells us a consistent drought began about 1276 and lasted for twenty-three years. Perhaps already stressed by population overshoot, that prolonged drought would have tightened the screw, gradually depleted the villages, either by starvation, disease, and/or the beginnings of a forced migration.

The term "sustainability" is in common use with modern environmentalists, and pretenders. Some of them truly understand it, but for others it is merely a code word for "sustainable development," a slight of hand used to justify continued growth. Primitive people—and in the long run us moderns as well—were (and are) constrained by what a modern biologist knows as "carrying capacity." Pressured by their own success in building populations, limited by primitive technologies and an unsustainable agriculture, the Mimbres culture was in no better position to survive a combination of population overshoot aggravated by drought than the populations of jackrabbits they sought for dinner. In the end not even perennial waters could save them, for the land and resources the waters nourished had been depleted, though hardly to the extent we have depleted them today.

Well before the Apache moved in—who most likely would have killed them off or driven them out in any event—the remaining Mimbres gradually moved on. As Calvin wrote: "No propitiation availed to bring back the harmony between man and sky and soil. All had failed, and in the failure the old men and the priests, interpreters of the wisdom of the Ancients, read the signal to depart."

It is not strictly true that they all just disappeared; it is more the case that we simply don't know where they went. They left lessons—and a rare art that held the story of their lives—never to be seen again.

Studio portrait of Geronimo. Image #000139; courtesy of the John Harlan Collection. The Silver City Museum, Silver City, New Mexico.

THREE

Equine Buccaneers

THE MOUNTAINS DRAW THE WATERS. THE WATERS DRAW THE PEOPLE. A century or two after the Mogollon peoples moved on, a rather different group of Native Americans came to call the Gila home. Athabaskan peoples, who shared language similarities with the Navajos, had a different way of finding sustenance. Having selected the wildest, most rugged terrain in the territory now called New Mexico had to offer, they readily took on the character of their surroundings. They were farmers incidentally, hunters seriously, and raiders and warriors by choice. They moved through the Gila, Mimbres, and San Francisco valleys, settling there at times, but never permanently. They were more at home in the mountains; the challenge of the Gila's awesome heights and declinations seems to have suited their temperament. They moved with the seasons, the game, or in accordance with who they were chasing, or who was chasing them. Their adaptability was fluid, for they could make a home, at least temporarily, from the peaks and canyons to the desert floor. Their carrying capacity in relation to the land was fluid too, for they were not just dependent on what they could grow, gather, or catch on their own—they did not hesitate to flourish off the booty of others. They were the Apaches.

In *Geronimo: His Own Story*, dictated to S. M. Barrett, Geronimo wrote, "In that country which lies around the headwaters of the Gila River I was reared. This range was our fatherland; among these mountains our wigwams were hidden; the scattered valleys contained our fields; the boundless prairies, stretching away on every side, were our pastures; the rocky caverns were our burying places."

He described how they lived and values he learned early:

> When we were old enough to be of real service we went to the field with our parents, not to play but to toil. When the crops were to be planted we broke the ground with wooden hoes. We planted the corn in straight rows, the beans among the corn, and the melons and pumpkins in irregular order over the field. We cultivated these crops as there was need.
>
> . . . Besides grinding the corn (by hand with stone mortars and pestles) for bread, we sometimes crushed it and soaked it, and after it had fermented made from this juice a "tis-win," which had the power of intoxication, and was very highly prized by the Indians . . . [W]hen berries or nuts were to be gathered the small children and the squaws would go in parties to hunt them, and sometimes stay all day. When they went a great distance from camp they took ponies to carry the baskets.

Geronimo said the Apaches reveled in the hunting pursuits, perhaps a prelude to raiding, which would come in time.

> When I was about eight or ten years old I began to follow the chase, and to me this was never work.
>
> Out on the prairies which ran up to our mountain homes wandered herds of deer, antelope, elk, and buffalo, to be slaughtered when we needed them . . . [I]t required more skill to hunt the deer than any other animal. We never tried to approach a deer except against the wind. Frequently we would spend hours in stealing upon grazing deer. If they were in the open we would crawl a long distance on the ground, keeping a weed or brush before us, so that our approach would not be noticed. Often we could kill several out of one herd before the others would run away.

More pleasures of the chase:

In the forests and along the streams were many wild turkeys.
These we would drive to the plains . . . until they were almost
tired out. When they began to drop and hide we would ride
in upon them and swinging from the side of our horses, catch
them. If one started to fly we would ride swiftly under him
and kill him with a short stick, or hunting club. In this way
we could usually get as many wild turkeys as we could carry
home on a horse.

Lest this sound fanciful, Theodore Roosevelt wrote of running
down wild turkeys horseback in much the same manner, because turkeys cannot fly great distances, only Roosevelt had greyhounds to help
with the coup de grace. And who today would have the horsemanship
to catch a jackrabbit like this: "There were many rabbits on our range,"
Geronimo wrote, "and we also hunted them on horseback. Our horses
were trained to follow the rabbit at full speed, and as they approached
them we would swing from one side of the horse and strike the rabbit
with our hunting club."

Hunting was a pleasure as well as a necessity, and a right of passage.
Even more so was reaching the age of battle.

In 1846, being seventeen years of age, I was admitted to the
council of the warriors. Then I was very happy, for I could go
wherever I wanted and do whatever I liked. I had not been
under the control of any individual, but the customs of our
tribe prohibited me from sharing the glories of the warpath
until the council admitted me. When opportunity offered,
after this, I could go on the warpath with my tribe. This would
be glorious. I hoped soon to serve my people in battle. I had
long desired to fight with our warriors.

Geronimo's story tells us much about the Apaches, it seems to me.
They *were* farmers to some extent; hunting was a sacred pleasure as well
as a necessity; war was a part of life and not to be feared—it was "glorious." It seems they liked it, but cautiously. Not in pitched battles where
they might lose, but with guile, and primarily to get stuff. By Geronimo's
time, it was part of life and learned from the ground up.

Geronimo's writings on war and raiding would seem to belie a common error of modern history, revisionist in tone and founded on white guilt—that the Apaches were a peaceful tribe of hunter/gatherers until European incursion forced them into warfare and piracy. Not all historians were so deluded. In *River of the Sun* Ross Calvin wrote, "Back in aboriginal times, long before the coming of the Mexican, Apaches had become accustomed to raiding the agricultural village of the Pimas with the cracking of none knows how many skulls." Walter Prescott Webb wrote in *The Great Plains*, "It seems safe to conclude that before the coming of the Spaniards the Apaches had already established a feud with the pueblo Indians of the Southwest. When the Spaniards came in they found little difficulty in working among these pueblo Indians. Soon they found themselves taking part with the Pimas and others against the raiding Apaches; therefore the Apaches made no distinction between the Spaniards and their old enemies—they raided all alike."

Then they got the horse. The Apache were the first *indios broncos* according to J. Frank Dobie, writing in *The Mustangs* that by 1630 they were "well mounted."

"They are on horseback from infancy," wrote Lt. William Emory, one of the first of the Anglo tribe to encounter the Apaches and leave a detailed written record, in *Notes of a Military Reconnaissance* (1848). This gave them the range to raid deep into Mexico and scare the bejesus out of Spanish/Mexican settlements as far south as Durango. By 1846, the year Geronimo joined the council of warriors, the Apaches were to the Southwest what the Comanches and Kiowas were to the South Plains—the ultimate equine buccaneers. An interesting portrait of that time—indeed the same year of 1846—was drawn by Lt. Emory. He was the scribe and natural historian of General Kearney's Army of the West that traveled along the Gila in hopeful conquest of California, part of the American government's self-made Mexican War. Where the Gila River has confluence with Mangas Creek (called Santa Lucia Creek then and near the present town of Cliff, New Mexico), the troop met up with a friendly band of Apaches. Their leader, of whom, sadly, no photo exists, is described in various historical accounts as standing "six-four" or "six-six," or "head and shoulders above every white man present." Before his death by American treachery in 1863, Mangas Colorados would become Geronimo's mentor in raiding, war, and leadership as the American army slowly ground down and corralled the remaining Apache forces. But there was no raid or warfare this day where Mangas Creek meets the Gila, rather a friendly trading party. Perhaps Geronimo was there; Lt. Emory doesn't say. But in his report he left this account of a lively Apache woman who, like Geronimo, was high-spirited, freewheeling, audacious, and a master at the acquisition of booty. With Lt. Emory's subsequent comments, and those of Geronimo himself, it seems these were tribal traits.

> Amongst them [the Apaches] was a middle-aged woman, whose garrulity and interference in every trade was the annoyance of Major Swords, who had charge of the trading, but the amusement of the by-standers.
>
> She had on a gauze-like dress, trimmed with the richest and most costly Brussel's lace, pillaged no doubt from some fandango-going belle of Sonora; (what the horrific fate of the Spanish girl who originally owned the dress might have been is anybody's speculation); she straddled a fine grey horse, and whenever her blanket dropped from her shoulders, her tawny form could be seen through the transparent gauze. After she had sold her mule, she was anxious to sell her horse, and careened about to show his qualities. At one time she charged full speed up a steep hill. In this, the fastenings of her dress broke, and her bare back was exposed to the crowd, who ungallantly raised a shout of laughter. Nothing daunted, she wheeled short round with surprising dexterity, and seeing the mischief done, coolly slipped the dress from her arms and tucked it between her seat and the saddle. In this state of nudity she rode through camp, from fire to fire, until at last, attaining the object of her ambition, a soldier's red flannel shirt, she made her adieu in that new costume.

Evidently, Apache horsemanship was not confined to the men. Covering up to one hundred miles a day, riding, stealing, trailing horses and mules (and eating a few as they needed them along the way), with a fine turn of phrase Emory noted for all time "the great stealing road of the Apaches." He elaborated:

Nature has done her utmost to favor a condition of things
which has enabled a savage and uncivilized tribe, armed with
bow and lance, to hold as tributary powers three fertile and
once-flourishing states, Chihuahua, Sonora and Durango,
peopled by a Christian race, countrymen of the immortal
Cortez. These states were at one time flourishing, but such has
been the devastation and alarm spread by these children of the
mountains, that they are now losing population, commerce
and manufacture at a rate which, if not soon arrested, must
leave them uninhabited.

According to Geronimo, raiding was hardly a crime, but a way of
life, something practiced with a kind of fierce joy, and the Mexicans at
times were not merely victims but willingly part of the game: "About a
year after this [1868]," Geronimo wrote,

Mexican troops rounded up all the horses and mules of the
tribe not far from our settlement. No raids had been made into
Mexico that year, and we were not expecting any attacks. We
were all in camp, having just returned from hunting.

About two o'clock in the afternoon two Mexican scouts
were seen near our settlement. We killed these scouts, but the
troops got under way with our herd of horses and mules before
we saw them. It was useless to try to overtake them on foot,
and our tribe had not a horse left. I took twenty warriors and
trailed them (on foot). We found the stock at a cattle ranch in
Sonora, not far from Nacozari, and attacked the cowboys who
had them in charge. We killed two men and lost none. After
the fight we drove off our own stock and all of theirs.

We were trailed by nine cowboys. I sent the stock on
ahead and with three warriors stayed in the rear to intercept
any attacking parties. One night when near the Arizona line
we discovered these cowboys on our trail and watched them
camp for the night and picket their horses. About midnight
we stole into their camp and silently led away all their horses,
leaving the cowboys asleep. Then we rode hard and overtook
our companions, who always traveled at night instead of in

the daytime. We turned these horses in with the herd and fell back to again intercept anyone who might trail us. What these nine cowboys did next morning I do not know, and I have never heard the Mexicans say anything about it; I know they did not follow us, for we were not molested. When we arrived in camp at home there was great rejoicing in the tribe. It was considered a good trick to get the Mexicans' horses and leave them asleep in the mountains.

Of course this was a game that could not last. After the Mexican War the American side of the international line (none of these borders meant anything to the Apaches, of course) began to fill up with Anglo as well as Mexican settlers. By 1877 the Plains tribes were pretty well confined and the American military could focus on the holdouts, the Apaches of the Southwest. When General George Crook took over from General Orlando Willcox, he began using reservation Apaches as scouts in his pursuits of Geronimo and other renegades. Some of these American military war parties had more Indians than whites fighting *with* the troopers; even the most remote hiding places in the Gila or Sierra Madre were now vulnerable. One of Geronimo's last holdouts was Teepee Canyon, a tributary of Mogollon Creek, itself a tributary of the Gila River in what is now the Gila Wilderness. Traces of their fires from their last winter may still be seen there. Raids, pursuits, and fights continued for years, but Crook was wearing them down.

In March 1886 Geronimo and his last renegades sued for peace. Or so they said. At their meeting in the Sierra Madre, he told Crook he would gather up the last of his scattered band, less than fifty Apaches and nearly half of them women and children, and bring them in to the reservation at San Carlos, Arizona. Crook took him at his word and left him there with that promise; when it wasn't kept and Geronimo returned to the mountains, Crook resigned his command. Geronimo should have gone with Crook. Six months later, when he finally surrendered to General Nelson Miles, he was clamped in irons with all the rest and sent by train to Florida.

The Battle of the Little Big Horn was *the* great Indian victory of the Indian wars, but within the year (1876) the Great Plains Indian wars were essentially over. It was another ten years before the Apaches succumbed, a tribute not only to the fighting powers and elusiveness of this particular strain of native, but to the forbidding mountains and mazelike terrain of the Gila and surrounding watersheds north and south of the Mexican line. Only the Apaches had grown up there and learned to live there on the run. Even the churchly Christian Ross Calvin, rector of the Church of the Good Shepherd of Silver City, where Apache depredations where still fresh in the mind in the 1920s, offered his grudging admiration, as he wrote in *Sky Determines,*

> History has persisted in misunderstanding the Apache. He has been viewed exclusively and constitutionally as an enemy, a sort of rattlesnake among men. Historians have taken up the word *apachu,* "enemy," which the timorous Zunis applied to him, and the name has stuck. To the unwarlike Pueblos, no doubt, these free-roving falcons of the desert were indeed enemies, but it is unfair to withhold a certain tribute of applause from the soaring hawk because he must get his living from buccaneering.

Certainly the Apaches retarded "settlement" of the Gila country by decades. Geronimo ended up at the reservation at Ft. Sill, Oklahoma, and lived into his eighties, but not long enough to ever see his homeland again. In 2006 descendents of the old warrior, with the cooperation of the National Park Service, erected a monument to Geronimo, "in that country that lies around the headwaters of the Gila River [where] I was reared."

Less well known is an unauthorized monument, now dismantled by the Forest Service, erected to the Apaches in the 1970s by a small group of outlaw environmentalists, the progenitors of Earth First! Set in the Gila Wilderness, it lauded the Apaches as the first defenders against unsavory development. It must have been great sport, roguish, essentially harmless, but inspiring and the stuff of legend. And I know it's true because I've seen the pictures of the construction in action; some of the participants are recognizable, are known to me, and may still be found in our state, albeit now leading somewhat respectable lives.

The headwaters of the Gila watershed, rugged beyond knowing in the way of the Apaches, have always resisted unsavory development. And, while buccaneering is now passé, its earlier defenders continue to inspire.

Nat Straw. Courtesy of the Silver City Museum, Silver City, New Mexico.

FOUR

Mountain Men and Other Characters

WITH HIS GRIP ON THE IMAGINATION, PSYCHE, AND NATIONAL CHARACTER, the mountain man rivals the cowboy as the archetypal American Hero. In the Southwest the mountain man reached his zenith, and held his lifestyle longest, in the region's last great wilderness—the Gila country of southwest New Mexico. Here within the mountains and canyons of the Gila, San Francisco, and Mimbres rivers, the mountain man era lasted well into the twentieth century. Indeed, I would submit that within mountain man mythology the region has been neglected historically. The northern Rockies may well have led the beaver trade in scope and commerce, but for color, character, and arduous mishaps, adventures, and (sometimes dubious) achievements, not even Jim Bridger or Brokenhand Fitzpatrick could exceed the wilderness high jinks of those Anglo adventurers who took to the mountains of the Gila as a way of life.

James Ohio Pattie

It was fur that brought the first mountain men west. From St. Louis trappers seeking beaver went northwest up the Missouri and Platte rivers, or south and west on the Santa Fe Trail to Taos, recently taken into the hands of Mexico from Spain. By the mid 1820s Taos was trappers' headquarters. In the fall of 1825 a group of trappers outfitted in Taos were determined to explore a new range of mountains beyond the desert to the south and west. Among them was a twenty-one-year-old of romantic notions named James Ohio Pattie (1804–?).

Pattie was from Kentucky and he was not, in retrospect, a great mountain man. He was only marginally successful as a trapper, nearly starved to death in the wilderness several times, and was once so foolish as to drop his gun in fright in the face of an angry grizzly bear. Yet he was with the first group of mountain men to explore the Gila drainage and is forever etched in mountain man history because he left a book detailing his adventures: *The Personal Narrative of James O. Pattie of Kentucky*.

Pattie's *Narrative* remains a fascinating document for the modern reader. Though not always accurate as to dates and chronology, Pattie gives the reader a vivid picture of pristine southwest New Mexico in the 1820s: the lush, riparian bosque near Socorro, where he encountered his first bear; the climb over the Black Range near Emory Pass and descent to Santa Rita del Cobre near present day Silver City; the descent of Sapillo Creek to the Gila River where the trappers took thirty beaver the first night. Here in a brief paragraph he gives a rare written glimpse of the Gila River as nature made it, describing the reach from Sapillo Creek upstream to the forks:

> On the morning of the 13th we started early, and crossed
> the river, here a beautiful clear stream about thirty yards in
> width, running over a rocky bottom, and filled with fish. We
> made but little advance this day, as bluffs came in so close to
> the river, as to compel us to cross it thirty-six times. We were
> obliged to scramble along under the cliffs, sometimes on our
> hands and knees, through a thick tangle of grape-vines and
> underbrush . . . [W]e were rejoiced when this rough ground
> gave place again to the level bottom. At night we reached a
> point, where the river forked, and encamped on the point
> between the forks. We found here a boiling spring so near the
> main stream that the fish caught in the one might be thrown
> into the other without leaving the spot, where it was taken.
> In six minutes it would be thoroughly cooked.

Today this stretch of the Gila is still rugged, requires numerous stream crossings, is somewhat less lush but improving, and features several well-known hot springs. Pattie was likely the first white man to catch and cook a Gila trout. While "endangered," this species is still present in portions of the Gila, and in good years the river is still "filled with fish," and with an even greater variety than Pattie could have found at the time.

Later, downriver, Pattie describes the river entering such a narrow canyon that they had to detour their horses and mules far to the south. The detour was arduous and they survived only by butchering one of their horses for food, and one time by eagerly devouring a jackrabbit caught by their camp dog. The modern reader recognizes the rugged Gila Middle Box Canyon; based on Pattie's description, it's changed but little. It is still impossible to get livestock down through the canyon; river runners attempt it, and some make it but not without a spill or two; and you can hike it at low water but only by wading or swimming the deeper pools as there are no banks, only canyon walls going straight up thirty feet. In places the "box" is only six feet across and a tall man can touch both walls with the span of his arms.

That first winter Pattie's party trapped down to the confluence of the San Francisco River, then up the "Frisco" until back into New Mexico. Beaver were plentiful, and he commented on the river and its bounty:

> We called it the river San Francisco. After traveling up its banks about four miles, we encamped, and set all our traps, and killed a couple of fat turkeys. In the morning we examined our traps, and found in them 37 beavers! This success restored our spirits instantaneously. Exhilarating prospects now opened before us, and we pushed on with animation. The banks of this river are for the most part incapable of cultivation being in many places formed of high and rugged mountains. Upon these we saw multitudes of mountain sheep. These animals are not found on level ground being there slow of foot, but on these cliffs and rocks they are so nimble and expert in jumping from point to point, that no dog or wolf can overtake them. One of them that we killed had the largest horns that I ever saw on animals of any description. One of them would hold a gallon of water.

As on the "Helay," as he called it, the trappers found the San Francisco a small but fierce canyon river and riparian jungle, bountiful in the midst of the surrounding desert.

From the two rivers they would total a sum exceeding 250 beaver, only to lose the cache, and one of the trappers, in encounters with Apaches. Persistent, Pattie and a few others made a similar foray the next winter (1826–1827). Again the "Helay," and the Frisco, would produce fur. They figured a total of some $20,000 worth of beaver, which they this time managed to pack to Santa Fe. Even divided up, it was a small fortune at the time. The furs were promptly confiscated in Santa Fe by the Mexican governor. Here Pattie commented in his diary: "The whole fruit of our long, toilsome and dangerous expedition was lost, and all of my golden hopes of prosperity and comfort vanished like a dream."

Pattie would make other forays into the Southwest wilderness, keeping his diary, often less accurately, along the way; his "Helay" portions carry his best historical contributions. His luck was good enough to survive all this adventure, but he was feckless in commerce and arrived back in the Midwest penniless, his health broken, but with a headful of experiences and the remnants of a diary that his vivid imagination sometimes overleapt. Fortunately for posterity, he promptly turned that dairy into the *Narrative*, imperfect but invaluable. Ever luckless in finance, James Ohio Pattie was never to profit from his book. In Cincinnati he got Timothy Flint of the *Western Historical Review* to publish the book, saw it in print in 1831, and must have had a brief fling with fame and celebrity, if not royalties. His days as an author were numbered. He simply disappears from history about 1833, probably the victim of a cholera epidemic.

James Kirker

Perhaps the most historically significant of the Gila mountain men was a contemporary of Pattie's named James Kirker (1793–1853). Kirker arrived at the Gila trappers' headquarters, the Santa Rita copper mines, in 1826, just one year after Pattie, and he stayed for a decade at least, trapping the Gila streams and acting as a guard, scout, and manager of the mines. By his own account (he was literate and some of his correspondence survived) Kirker was "highly successful" as a trapper. According to

James Kirker. Courtesy of M. H. Salmon.

William C. McGaw, author of *Savage Scene: The Life and Times of James Kirker, Frontier King*, Kirker was once gone off in the Gila wilderness, hunting and trapping, for eighteen months. As late as 1837, when beaver were of lesser economic consequence due to their scarcity and changes in fashion, Kirker emerged from the Gila with more than a thousand beaver pelts, only to lose the entirety, like Pattie, to an Indian raid.

But Kirker would be of minor historical interest had his career ended with beaver trapping. Instead, following the Apache uprising of 1837, Kirker turned to a more lucrative pursuit: scalp hunting. Hiring out to the Mexican government for $200 per scalp—a ferocious sum at the time— Kirker led vigilantes of fifty to one hundred men, many of them Shawnee and Delaware Indians, on punitive expeditions against the Apaches. The scourge lasted a half dozen years and ranged over the wilderness from Taos to Santa Rita to Chihuahua City. The toll of the Apache dead eventually exceeded five hundred, the scalps hung in gruesome display in the Ciudad Chihuahua square. One of Kirker's recruits, James Hobbs, wrote, "We would fight certain tribes . . . for the fun of the thing, and for common humanity, even if we were not rewarded for every scalp."

This was *Blood Meridian* long before Cormac McCarthy thought to invent it. Yet Kirker survived it all—the wilderness trapping, the Indian wars, the Mexican War (1846), where he served the American forces as a scout—to die of natural causes in 1853 in California. His legacy, however, remains in the Gila.

While living in Santa Rita, between expeditions into the Gila River country, he married an El Paso woman and started a family near the copper mines. He would father seven children in that locale before abandoning the family and taking a powder for new adventures. The family remained behind; many worked for generations at the copper mines (some still do) and the region still boasts dozens who carry the Kirker name, all descended from a fierce reprobate who first came to the area to trap the Gila's beaver in 1826.

James "Bear" Moore

For a period following the decline in the beaver trade the mountain man as a type faded from the Southwest. He reemerged in the latter part of the nineteenth century in the form of a number of remarkable wilderness

"Me and that bear had it right there." —James "Bear" Moore.
Courtesy of the Fredric Remington art museum.

adventurers who hunted predatory animals. Not surprisingly, these wild men of the mountains picked the wildest country they could find, the headwaters of the Gila, San Francisco, and Mimbres rivers, where the last of what were thought of at the time as "noxious animals" were, in the days preceding game laws, holding out.

The term "mountain man" gets thrown around a lot in the current outdoor media. In some quarters, it seems all you have to do to earn the title "mountain man" is spend a few nights camped out and grow a stubble beard. For me, a mountain man is a person who has made the mountains home. He doesn't adventure there; he *lives* in the wilderness, making an occasional trip to town for supplies or society. The Gila country has held some of the great and infamous mountain men of the

West, but to my knowledge there is not a single mountain man in the Gila today; the myth survives, the history and the spirit, but the grit and yen for prolonged hermitage seems to have passed.

By any measure, James "Bear" Moore was a true mountain man. From the early 1880s to his death in January 1924, he spent the better part of his time camped out in remote areas of southwest New Mexico. Unlike fellow mountain men and contemporaries, like Nat Straw, who was gregarious and a storyteller, or Ben Lilly, who rather liked all the publicity he received, Bear Moore was fearful of society. And he could be fearsome to anyone who tried to enter his self-imposed solitude. His desire for anonymity was largely successful; I know of no photo of Bear Moore, and all that is known about him can be contained in one short newspaper column.

Among those who knew Moore and left a record of it was Jack Stockbridge, as reported by Elizabeth McFarland in *Wilderness of the Gila*. He befriended Moore when the mountain man was living in a cave along Turkey Creek in the early 1900s. Stockbridge said that at that time Bear Moore appeared to be about fifty years old, and that Moore told him the following story of how he got the nickname "Bear."

> In 1892, I'd gone over in the San Mateo's to see a friend. I always used one of them old Sharp's 45–70 single shot rifles. About a mile from the cabin where I was staying, I went hunting with that old rifle and I run on to a little young bear up a tree. I shot it but didn't kill it, and it squawked and fell out of that tree.
>
> About that time here comes the old she bear. I went to jump back out of the way and fell backwards over a log with the bear right on top of me. As I fell, I lost my gun, but I always carry a bowie knife. Me and that bear had it right there. The bear got a hold of me and bit me through the jaws and on my forehead and through my arms and clawed me acrost the breast. That bear just darn near chewed me up and spit me out.
>
> I managed to kill the bear with my bowie knife, and crawled back a mile to the cabin where my friend was. He taken me in to Magdalena to the hospital and they patched me up there as best they could. My face was left all twisted out to one side and I never shaved after that. I can't talk

very plain either. There's scars on my forehead and arms, and you can see my heart beat where that bear clawed my chest open.

When I was able, they sent me back to my home in Missouri and I stayed there until I was cured up enough to come back out here again. Ever since, they've always called me Bear Moore.

An article in the July 2, 1892, Silver City *Enterprise* largely confirms this tale. The news story, without a byline, says that Moore was brought into St. Vincent's hospital, describes the injuries much as Moore did to Stockbridge, and said that, "Dr. Longwell sewed up all his wounds yesterday afternoon, and he displayed splendid nerve."

Now disfigured, Bear Moore became a confirmed recluse and drifted deeper into the wilds of the Gila, killing his own meat, selling a few hides, even raising a crop and keeping a few hogs during a long period when he had a homestead camp along the west fork of the Gila River. (A remnant of his cabin there survives.) From time to time he would bring in some gold dust to Pinos Altos or Silver City that he would trade for salt, ammunition, or other supplies. This gold was a small portion of what some say was Bear Moore's mother lode. In later years, Jack Stockbridge explained where this gold came from.

"Bear Moore got to looking around," Stockbridge said, "and he found a pretty good quartz vein that runs out through Ring Canyon and breaks out into red bluffs right across the West Fork [of the Gila] from Chicken Coop Canyon."

Legend has it that Bear Moore mined a fortune of gold out of that quartz vein. If so, nobody but Moore ever saw it. Legend also has it that others since have sought that mother lode in Ring Canyon. If anyone found it, they were very quiet about getting it out.

Meanwhile, Moore waged a vendetta against that tribe of animals, bears, that had disfigured him. He built massive log bear traps, homegrown cages if you will, some of which may still be found in the Gila Wilderness. Once he had lured a bear into the trap with food, he dropped the trap door and lashed out at a bad memory. Jack Stockbridge once witnessed the cruelty: "I heard the durndest racket . . . and rode down and there was Bear Moore with a bowie knife tied onto a stout stick, poking between the logs of a trap at the bear . . . and he kept on that way until he killed the bear."

The death of Bear Moore was the finality of the hard life of a hard man. According to Harry Watson, longtime resident of Pinos Altos, the body of Bear Moore was found by the dogs of predator-hunter Homer Pickens early in February 1924 on the west side of Brushy Mountain. Only Pickens didn't know who he had found. Pickens rode to Alum Camp along the Gila River where he met Watson who was set up for a hunt. He told Watson about the body and said, "I think it's Ben Lilly, but I don't know."

Watson doubted it was Lilly, saying, "Lilly isn't in this country now." He said Bear Moore wintered around Brushy Mountain and agreed to go with Pickens the next day to try to identify the body. He later reported,

> About six miles from Alum Camp, on the west side of Brushy Mountain, looking toward Little Creek, I found a camp before I seen the body. I got down off the horse and found a gold-pan laying there. I turned it over and there was Bear Moore's notebook with some little accounts that he had here and there. He was a very well educated man and wrote a beautiful hand.
>
> Then I saw the body and it was Bear Moore all right. The body was well preserved lying half buried in a bank of snow. He had evidently been caught in that big heavy snowstorm five weeks before . . .
>
> . . . He'd got out between two big pine trees and built him a little fire and had a few beans and some tallow in a little pot. He had the carcass of a couple of deer hanging up there and a few steaks had been hacked off. In order to keep his fire going, Bear Moore had walked over to a fallen pine tree with his axe to get some pitch-rich pine wood. Evidently he fell over the log to the far side and never got up again.

Bear Moore was buried close to where he died. A true mountain man, and one of the last, on February 8, 1924, the *Enterprise* wrote, "He chose his life's work and was found cold in death on duty."

In recent years a small brass plaque has been placed near the death site, reading: Bear Moore R.I.P.

Ben Lilly

Historian Frederick Jackson Turner declared the frontier closed in 1890. Other historians and writers see the Old West lingering until 1900 or even 1910. The date that marks the end of western history is in dispute, but all enthusiasts of the Old West remain fascinated by those westerners who carried the lifeways and myths of the era into a more modern time.

For example, Ben Kilpatrick, a prominent member of Butch Cassidy's Wild Bunch around the turn of the century, attempted an Old West train robbery near Sanderson, Texas, in 1912. He got his skull crushed with an ice mallet for his troubles. With World War I well underway and trucks and planes and artillery rapidly taking the day, Pancho Villa and five hundred mounted guerrillas raided Columbus, New Mexico, in 1916. General John "Black Jack" Pershing's futile pursuit of Villa into Mexico would be the last major campaign of the U.S. Cavalry.

And then there is the legend and lore of the mountain man. Within the genre of mountain man history, Benjamin Vernon Lilly exemplifies the western character who lived, and thrived, beyond his time. Inevitably, he would end up around the headwaters of the Gila watershed, that place remaining equal to his wildness and eccentricities.

Born in 1856 in Alabama, Ben Lilly was a legend in the Old South before he ever went west. Living for extended periods in his home state, as well as Mississippi and Louisiana, he tried farming, logging, cattle trading, and marriage, with a roughly equal lack of success. What he could do well was hunt. Stocking the family larder with deer, squirrel, or rabbit was of lesser interest to Lilly, merely a pastime of the rural life of the period. His passion was bears and mountain lions, generally called panthers in the South, which he trailed through the shrinking southern wilderness with remarkable skill and perseverance, and with the aid of trailing hounds that would become his signature as a hunter. Rabid in the pursuit of game for weeks, even months, at a time, his extended hunts were the main reason his farming, logging, cattle trading, and two marriages ultimately ended in failure.

One story handed down from Ben Lilly's early days in the South has his wife handing him his gun and telling him to go shoot the hawk that had been stealing the chickens. Ben Lilly, it is said, returned from the hunt many months (some say a whole year) later. "That hawk kept flying," he told his wife.

Ben Lilly, 1906, when he was about fifty years old. Photo by John Strickrott.
Courtesy of M. H. Salmon.

It is certain that over the years Ben Lilly kept a hunting journal in which he recorded his catches. By the turn of the century, according to his own notes, he had killed 120 bears and about half as many lions. But the Southern frontier was being taken by settlement and few of the great predators remained in the southern wilderness. Sixteen years after Turner declared the frontier closed, Ben Lilly was about to reinvent the western myth in his own image. Lilly's biographer, J. Frank Dobie, captures the moment in *The Ben Lilly Legend*.

> Early in 1906, with no more in his purse than an apostle is supposed to have, with no scrip at all, and seemingly with a mind made up never to return home, Ben Lilly, soon to be fifty years old, entered the Big Thicket of Texas against the Louisiana line. Thenceforth he was to be as detached geographically as he had always been inwardly from the tie-ropes of family and home opinion. There is no evidence he ever wanted or ever had a fling with wine, women, or song. He wanted to live stark free of all human restraints—and to hunt. He wore his beard, drank water, lived on squirrel meat and corn bread, and went his wonted way.

Ben Lilly would have one final fling as a famed hunter in the Old South. In 1907 he was called east from Texas to the Tensas Bayou of Louisiana to help President Theodore Roosevelt kill a bear. The president, not easily impressed by men, would later recall Lilly this way:

> . . . spare, full bearded, with mild, gentle, blue eyes and a frame of steel and whipcord. I never met any other man so indifferent to fatigue and hardship. He equaled Cooper's *Deerslayer* in woodcraft, in hardihood, in simplicity—and also in loquacity. The morning he joined us in camp, he had come on foot through the thick woods, followed by his two dogs, and had neither eaten nor drunk for twenty-four hours; for he did not like to drink the swamp water. It had rained hard throughout the night and he had no shelter, no rubber coat, nothing but the clothes he was wearing, and the ground was too wet for him to lie on; so he perched in a crooked tree in

the beating rain, much as if he had been a wild turkey. But he
was not in the least tired when he struck camp; and, though
he slept an hour after breakfast, it was chiefly because he had
nothing else to do, inasmuch as it was Sunday, on which day
he never hunted or labored. He could run through the woods
like a buck, was far more enduring, and quite as indifferent to
weather, though he was over fifty years old. He had trapped
and hunted throughout almost all the half century of his
life, and on trail of game he was as sure as his own hounds.
His observations on wild creatures were singularly close
and accurate.

But Ben Lilly's pursuits lay west. He drifted across south Texas,
hunting and trapping for the sale of meat, hides, and pelts, and in 1908
entered Mexico, gradually working his way into the Sierra Madre along
the Chihuahua/Sonora border. He hired out to provide remote mining
operations with camp meat, and for the first time he found people—in
the form of cattle ranchers—who would pay him to kill predatory animals. What he had formerly done at a loss would hence become a profit-
able life's work.

Ben Lilly spent about two years in the Sierra Madre of Mexico, add-
ing to a growing total of black bears and mountain lions killed. For the
first time in his hunting career he tracked to their doom several grizzly
bears, the ultimate challenge to the western houndman and his dogs.
He worked his way north and entered southwest New Mexico early in
1911. In March of that year, on one of his most memorable hunts, and
with just one young hound as companion on the trail, he chased a big
male grizzly to its ultimate, inevitable defeat. It began when the grizzly
stepped in one of Ben Lilly's bear traps near the Old Mexico line. The
description of the end of the hunt is taken from the hunter's own notes.

The brown grizzly with two toes off his front foot was still
missing. I went back after him, killed a female lion on the route,
and found that he had taken my trap. He traveled a rough
country, dragging the trap over rocks. He wore the chain and
the clog off the trap. I followed him for several days, into Sonora
and back into Chihuahua. He was making for his New Mexico

range when I killed him late on a Saturday evening. I had chased him in three states and two countries. His front tusks were worn to the gums, both above and below. That was why he had trouble killing cattle. He was the oldest bear I ever killed. The biological survey people called him a Nelson grizzly.

North of the New Mexico "bootheel," where Ben Lilly killed the Nelson grizzly, lies a vast range of wilderness mountains that are today part of the Gila and Apache-Sitgreaves national forests of New Mexico and Arizona and the headwaters of the Gila watershed. In this range in the early decades of the twentieth century was a remnant of frontier that was the equal to Ben Lilly's relentless pursuit of the wild. He would stay in these mountains for the remaining quarter century of his life, creating new chapters in a burgeoning career of western legend, lore, and history.

Whereas other hunters of the time lived at a base camp or ranch, making trips into the wilderness for a hunt, Ben Lilly lived in the wilderness, making an occasional trip back to a base camp for fresh dogs and supplies. His adventures in the wilds of the Gila drainage, and exploits and eccentricities, were common campfire talk long after he was gone. J. Frank Dobie collected many of these stories in his excellent book. Like many others, I read *The Ben Lilly Legend*, and over the years I read the recollections of others who had known Lilly, but I wasn't content with the reading. What I wanted to do was talk to someone who had known Ben Lilly and who had actually hunted with him.

By the time I arrived in southwest New Mexico in 1980, such remnants of the frontier were scarce, an endangered species about to fade forever from the scene. Time after time, one old-timer or another would tell me, "No, I didn't know him, but I saw him a time or two, when he'd come into town." Or, "No, I never hunted with Ben Lilly, but I knew him some; talked to him several times at the county poor farm where he went after he got senile." That wasn't what I wanted.

Then I met Jack Hooker, well into his eighties, but still lucid and interested in life. He and his wife had recently retired from their ranch and had come to a little place outside Silver City, New Mexico, to watch what was left of life go by. Mrs. Hooker poured coffee and Jack Hooker started to talk and for the next hour I had my living link to the last of the mountain men.

Yeah, I hunted with him; I knew Ben Lilly pretty good. I'd
ride and he'd walk alongside as fast as any horse and he'd talk
faster than that. Talk all day. He'd have half a dozen hounds
anyway, and he didn't tie his dogs; they obeyed him. When the
race would start and go to rough country, you couldn't keep
up with him. The first time I went with Ben Lilly I went afoot,
like him. That was a mistake. I was in my twenties then, and
he was past sixty, but when the race started and the hounds
went over the mountain, Lilly walked me down. After that
I rode a horse when I hunted with Ben Lilly.

Hooker also remembered Lilly's artistic talents.

He was an artist. He was always making hunting horns to
call his hounds in. With the point of his knife he would mark
out little dots on the horn that would come out a bear or lion.
Beautiful work. And he could make a knife overnight, right
there in camp. Made them out of a trap spring, tempered in a
campfire, always sharpened on both sides. I gave all my Lilly
knives away over the years. I wish I had one now to show you.
He was an artist with a knife.

Jack Hooker recalled that Lilly's favorite camp in the Gila Wilderness
was a cave about a mile up Sapillo Creek from its junction with the
Gila River.

I was little more than a boy. We were working cattle along
the Sapillo and camped along the Gila. Ben Lilly would
come down to our camp now and again, talk a blue streak
whether you answered back or not, then disappear. In a
blizzard one day down there we lost our horses. Myself and
some other boys found some of Ben Lilly's burros. He always
had real nice burros to help him move camp. We had to get
out of that blizzard so we rode his burros into Silver City and
a deputy took us in for stealing Ben Lilly's burros. He put
the burros in the pound. Later, Ben Lilly walked in from the
Sapillo to get his burros. He told the sheriff to let us go; he

didn't care if we borrowed his burros, blizzard or not. That deputy was going to make a name for himself catching us with Ben Lilly's burros, but he didn't get it done. We boys thought Ben Lilly was all right.

Later Jack Hooker had his own ranch along the nearby Mimbres River. Along with other ranchers in the area, he paid Ben Lilly a hundred dollars per lion as bounty. In *The Ben Lilly Legend*, J. Frank Dobie wrote that by 1928 Ben Lilly had "ceased to be very active." Jack Hooker remembers things differently.

Hell, he got five lions in one month off our ranch alone in 1929. That was too much; no lion was worth a hundred dollars in 1929. That was an awful lot of money then. The last one was the worst. The deal was, whoever had the ranch where the lion was killed, he paid the bounty. One day Ben's dogs treed a lion on a neighbor's ranch. Ben shot the lion but only wounded it. It baled out and ran a good ways before they treed it again. That second tree was on our ranch. Ben killed the lion out of that second tree, so we owed him the hundred dollars. That was too much. We let Ben go and I started to build my own pack. Used some of Ben's dogs too.

Jack Hooker told me that lion hunting had changed since Ben Lilly's time. "Nowadays a lion hunter may have a four-wheel drive truck and a snowmobile to help catch a lion. That's not how Ben Lilly did it. You don't learn about lions or hunting, driving around. Ben Lilly was the best because he was at home in the wilds, as much as any hound or varmint."

After Ben Lilly was gone, Jack Hooker remembered his cave along Sapillo Creek; "I knew he had buried something just outside the mouth of that cave. I always wondered what it was—a knife maybe, money? I was down there one time and I dug it up. It was the grave of one of his best hounds, ever. He buried Crook there and on the lid of a shoebox in pencil he wrote this out." Jack Hooker handed me the cover of the shoe box. You could still read it. In long hand, more elegant than grammatical, Lilly had written:

> Here lies Crook, a bear and lion dog that helped kill 210 bear
> and 426 lion since 1914 owned by B. V. Lilly. He died here the
> first Tuesday night in February 1925. He was owned and raised
> in camp and died in camp here. B. V. Lilly February 1925.

Ben Lilly at the height of his powers, with Crook and his other hounds, had killed 210 bears and 426 lions over a span of eleven years. To this day, enthusiasts of trailing dogs generally consider him to be the greatest houndman who ever lived.

Ben Lilly was a hunter at home in the wilderness into the early days of the Great Depression, eschewing the modern conveniences of home and hearth, and the mechanized pursuit and contraptions of the modern hunter, until his last hunt. By 1934, however, his mind had begun to leave him and he was taken to the county home near Pleasanton, New Mexico, along Big Dry Creek, just upstream of the San Francisco River. He died in December 1936, a few days shy of his eightieth birthday. To the end he wandered the hills near the old folks home, seeing imaginary lions and bears and calling to his hounds, long gone, by name, till that last day when he took to his bed and succumbed, saying, "I'll be better off."

J. Frank Dobie's *Legend* remains in print through the University of Texas Press. Therein is the both the history and the tall tales of the last of the mountain men, but what of the legacy?

Ben Lilly's prowess as a hunter of the big predators remains unequaled, though his lack of restraint cannot be reconciled within any conservation ethic. Like the buffalo hunters that preceded him, Ben Lilly never recognized that by annihilating his quarry, rather than merely selectively hunting it, he was destroying his own way of life.

His peculiarities continue to fascinate. He hunted on foot when everyone else out west was horseback. He would roll up in a hide during a snowstorm rather than accept a warm bed inside a cabin or house. He would not hunt or labor on Sunday, and if his hounds treed a lion on the Lord's Day he would refuse to kill it (though back there in the wilderness only the Lord could have known) until the Lord's Day had passed.

Most remarkable perhaps, he went west in the twentieth century at an age when most men are thinking about putting their feet up by the fire, and proceeded to create and maintain his own ethos within the western myth. A man out of time and a singular figure in western history, he reopened the frontier, or what was left of it, in the watershed of the wild Gila River. In the parting words of his biographer: "He came from a solitary race."

Tom Wood: A Grudge on the West Fork

He was a mountain man all right, known as "Hunter Tom Wood." Some people relied on him for skins, hides, and wild meat. For a price, of course. But he was a homesteader as well, with a place in the upper head-waters of the Gila, near Iron Creek, about as far from a road as you could get, then or now, and this would include anywhere in New Mexico. He too had a bear story from his youth.

According to an article in the Silver City *Enterprise*: "Wood narrowly escaped death in the jaws of a silver tip [grizzly bear]. The bear struck Wood on the side of the head, gouging out an eye and inflicting scars which he bore for the remainder of his life. As the bear stood over Wood, [George] Parker shot the bear and it fell dead across Wood's body."

Parker, a black man, would prove a good partner to Wood. In 1877 a particularly vicious outlaw gang, the Nelson Bunch, had a headquarters nearby, also back in the Gila near the headwaters of Sycamore Creek. Notorious horse and cattle thieves, they were also implicated in more than a dozen murders. Perhaps because they knew the country so well, and had a reputation for fearlessness, Wood and Parker were officially, or unofficially, deputized by Grant County Sheriff Harvey Whitehill to eviscerate what they could of this outlaw gang.

They did know the country, including the exact spot of the remote hideout. They staked it out and found a lone occupant—the remainder of the Nelson gang was off stealing stock in Arizona. As noted in an article by historian Jan Devereaux, also based on newspaper accounts, "They captured, bound and gagged him. Then they settled in to wait. Their patient surveillance paid its dividend."

The rest of this vigilante work comes straight from the *Enterprise*: "He [Bob Nelson] arrived at the cabin with a companion known as Portuguese Joe a little ahead of the five other men. Wood and Parker fired from close range, Parker killing the Portuguese, while Wood missed Nelson. Nelson fired a second shot, which also went wild, and as he tried to escape was shot from his horse and killed by Wood. The

remainder of the gang didn't put up much of a fight and three of them
were killed, two escaping."

Tom Wood was known from then on as a man-killer; he was already
a vigilante, hunter, and near victim of a grizzly bear, in many ways a
known quantity with a reputation both feared and respected on the
frontier. But life in the wilderness was really all he wanted, along with
wanting mostly to be left alone with his family, for this mountaineer had
a domestic side. As a mountain man, Tom Wood lived in the wilderness, but he wasn't a roamer in the way of Pattie, Lilly, or Nat Straw. He
brought a young Hispanic wife to his camp, Tomasita Cisneros, who left
a traveling circus to join him there. They built a cabin on Iron Creek,
just across Turkeyfeather Pass from the upper west fork of the Gila, had
a garden, hunted, fished and trapped, raised some stock and three children. The middle one, a son named Charley, had his father's flair for
dangerousness. By all accounts this was a family that preferred the wilderness life and had largely solved its hardships.

Into the midst of this wilderness tranquility, in 1885, came the
Grudgings brothers, Henry, Willie, and Charley, who built a cabin
and established a homestead of their own along the west fork, not far
upstream from what is now a national park, the Gila Cliff Dwellings, but
at the time as nearly remote a locale as Tom Wood's "property" further
up in the mountains. The Gila National Forest encompasses more than
three million acres; the west fork alone is more than thirty miles long.
You would think there was room for more than one homestead, one
cattle range, and at least several mountain man personalities, however
independent. Apparently not.

The Grudgings brothers were cattle rustlers, according to more than
one report, including the say-so of Tom Wood who threatened to expose
them. Meanwhile the Grudgingses had it on record, they claimed, that
Charley Wood, now fifteen, would butcher a Grudgings steer, jerk the
meat in the arid mountains, and sell it as deer jerky at substantial profit
on the streets of Silver City. However vast the wilderness and long the
river, a family feud developed, and they knew how to find each other.

On October 10, 1892, Charley Wood, returning with supplies on a
pack train from Silver City, made camp along the west fork, well above
the Grudgingses' cabin. His body was found there in camp the next day
by a passerby. Head lacerations suggested he had been pistol whipped

before being shot through the head. Nothing was stolen—the pack stock, burros, and supplies were still in camp. There were no suspects, but one could easily intuit a motive of hate.

Physical evidence was lacking, but in time Tom Wood focused on the Grudgings, and Willie Grudgings in particular became the marked man. The family feud was already there; the "grudge" preceding the killing. Rumors fly, even in the wilderness, and a dying cowboy, bucked off a horse and breathing his last, claimed he was there when it happened. It was Willie, he said, who killed fifteen-year-old Charley Wood. Or so some said he said.

Tom Wood had his reasons; *he*, at least, thought he had the crime solved. He would deliver his own justice. Whoever did it was foolish, for he had killed the son of a man with a reputation. On October 8, 1893, Tom Wood shot and killed Willie Grudgings outside by the corrals at the Grudgingses' homestead. Within days he had turned himself into the law, said he did it because Willie Grudgings had "killed my son." Held at Cooney, a tiny mining town with a cracker-box jail, he promptly slipped back into the wilderness and hung about the homestead for the better part of three years. As historian Devereaux notes, it's likely that with Tom Wood's reputation, nobody wanted to try and arrest him, especially on his home ground.

But on the lam Tom Wood was not a free man, and that, rather than guilt, may have weighed on the mental wellness of a lover of the wild. In 1896 he surrendered again, got a good lawyer, or at least a better one than the prosecutor, and was acquitted. He'd said he did it. Did the jury find him innocent, or simply justified? The record is silent. He returned to his mountain home and lived most of the remainder of his life there, seemingly content with the history he had already created, and died of natural causes at seventy-eight.

Willie Grudgings was buried by his brothers near the family homestead. The cabin remained long after the U.S. Forest Service took over the property, but burned in a forest fire in 1991. A headstone remains along the west fork for those who can find it:

WILLIAM GRUDGINGS
Waylaid and Murdered
By

Tom Wood
October 8, 1893
Age 37
Years 8 Months

Charley Wood is also buried deep in the Gila Wilderness, not far from
Gila waters on what was the family homestead. It all seems quite odd
today. I was up in the region of the Grudgings headstone just this past
summer fly-fishing for trout. Barring the rare flood, it would be hard
to find a more idyllic flow or peaceful locale for today's hikers, fishers, bird watchers, and horsemen who travel and enjoy it than the wilderness waters of the west fork of the Gila River. Near this flow, Willie
Grudgings rests quiet and cryptic in a bucolic park. Yet long ago that
pristine flow was witness to a pistol whipping, a murder, and revenge
that might have equaled the crime.

Nat Straw

Perhaps the last living link to the mountain man era in the Southwest
was Robert Nelson "Nat" Straw (1856–1941).

I first heard of Nat Straw many years ago. He was a man of the forest
and had legendary status as a trapper and hunter, right along with other
Gila mountain men like James Ohio Pattie, James Kirker, Montague
Stevens, and Ben Lilly. But where these other mountain men had books
written about them—and Stevens wrote his own—Straw seemed beyond
the reach of solid history. A few old-timers' reminiscences were all we
had, and their reliability was questioned. Some of this unreliability
came from Straw himself; he was a noted raconteur and had fun with
what Huck Finn called "stretchers." Fortunately, a modern biographer,
Carolyn O'Bagy Davis, finally tracked him down, and in 2004 penned
Mogollon Mountain Man: Nat Straw—Grizzly Hunter and Trapper.

In later years Nat Straw would claim to be from Minnesota and
Missouri, among other places, but never from Quebec, Canada. Davis's
research indicates that is just where Nat Straw was born, and she specu-
lates, reasonably I think, that Straw did not want to let on that his U.S.
citizenship may have been in doubt.

Three other periods of Straw's early years remain hazy, albeit rife with adventure. Straw always claimed that as a boy he was captured by the Sioux Indians and lived among them for about a year. Evidence is sketchy but acquaintances later reported that Straw did have knowledge of that Native American tongue.

He reported to old-timer Jack Stockbridge that as a teen he worked for a time with a cattle drive in eastern New Mexico. There he befriended Andy Adams, author of *The Log of a Cowboy*, a classic from the trail-driving era. Sure enough, one of the characters in Adams's book is named Nat Straw.

Finally, part of the Straw legend is that he lived with the Navajos for several years during the 1880s and that he fathered two daughters with his Navajo "wife."

But for all of the reports Straw left behind regarding his sometimes intemperate youth, solid evidence is lacking. And since Straw did at times undeniably tell tall tales, in the realm of the Pecos Bill or Paul Bunyan stories, his credibility was always suspect. But I found Nat Straw's memoirs of his early years believable. When Straw told a windy, as for example the story of Geronimo, the bear he saddled and rode, it was obvious. Both he and his listeners knew it was in fun. His early tales of Indians and cow camps, however, do not ring fantastic, but literal. My guess is he was really there.

Nat Straw was certainly there in the mountains of the Gila by the late 1880s, and he would spend the rest of his life in this wilderness. Davis records that he started out as a cowhand and camp cook but soon found a new calling. Davis writes,

> Eventually, he quit cowboying and became a professional hunter and trapper, working for the large ranches. Nat hunted for the V Cross T, the Flying V on the Middle Fork, and for Abb Alexander at the N-Bar Ranch. Porter, one of the bosses of the V Cross T, had seen cows with their hides torn and shredded by bears. He offered a ten dollar bounty for the predators, and soon had a room full of grizzly bear hides.

Nat Straw brought in some of those hides, but he didn't do it like Montague Stevens or Ben Lilly, both of whom were houndmen. Straw traveled the wilderness on foot, with burros to carry his camp, and he

got most of his bears, lions, and wolves by trapping. Davis reports that
Straw's grizzly bear traps weighed forty-two pounds and were both difficult and dangerous to set. He used some intriguing scent concoctions
to lure game to his traps, including that of a woman who was living on
the V Cross T ranch and was "unwell." Davis writes,

> Nat got the urine of the menstruating woman and created a
> very successful hunting scent. He recalled that throughout
> that year that he was working for the V Cross T, he trapped
> thirty-two wolves. Later on he met the daughter of a shop
> owner in Pinos Altos . . . The young woman showed Nat
> close up photographs she had taken of a wolf one day when
> she was walking in the nearby mountains. She said the wolf
> had acted very strangely. It seemed quite tame and had come
> very close to her. She did not know what had tamed the wolf,
> but Nat knew.

Davis's book is filled with the lore known only to those who have
lived in the mountains. In interviews with J. Frank Dobie, which Davis
wisely made liberal use of, Straw tells of longhorn steers, the only livestock that he claimed would "not give way" to the grizzly bear. He tells
of the grizzly that attacked a prospector armed with a pick. The bear
killed the miner but, badly wounded by the pick, was later tracked to his
doom by Straw. The recounting of Straw trapping a jaguar in the Black
Range in 1906 rings true and is of value to modern biologists who speculate about the big cat's historic range. Straw always camped near a Gila
stream, Davis reports, so he could please and feed himself catching wild
trout. This is believable because it makes such good sense, and also tells
us something about the Gila as a fishery in those early years.

Several Nat Straw stories are reprinted verbatim, as told to J. Frank
Dobie. The story of the grizzly and the zigzag trail is chilling and believable. The story of Nat's saddle-bear Geronimo is pure fiction but fun
to read. In the late 1930s, after more than forty years in the mountains,
Nat Straw walked from Gila Hot Springs to a farm outside Cliff, where
he spent his last years telling stories, smoking his pipe, and nipping at a
bottle of cheap whiskey by the banks of the Gila River. By then the wolf
and the grizzly were virtually gone from New Mexico, but there is no

evidence that Nat Straw ever acquired a conservation ethic. With the exception of Montague Stevens, a rancher and houndman who penned the markedly intelligent *Meet Mr. Grizzly*, the perspicuity required to see that you must not destroy what you love, especially as it gets scarce, never touched the Gila mountain men. It is the sad truth buried beneath the myths, campfire talk, and livid western tales that continue to fascinate.

Yet Nat Straw knew fishing, hunting, trapping, and wildlife beyond any modern man, and knew the Gila country with an intimacy that no one has duplicated since. He had much to teach, and one wishes, like Huckleberry Finn, that some of his "stretchers" were toned with wisdom.

Martin Price: The "Gila Monster"

Maybe Nat Straw was not the last of the Gila mountain men, but can a character be a mountain man in the modern day? After all, the Gila is as big today, and as unpopulated, as it was back then. Well maybe. But not without some trouble.

While a correspondent for the Albuquerque *Journal*, I spent an afternoon in the Grant County Jail interviewing a modern-day mountain man. This wasn't writing; it was just a matter of getting the man to talk and then arranging the notes so it all made some sense. After the piece came out there was some comment by law enforcement that I'd made the guy out to be better than he was. For example, I found out later that the man had kept a diary in which there were allusions to kidnapping some young and unsuspecting nubile and keeping her there in the wilderness so he could "raise her up right." Also, the man did not, to put it mildly, keep a clean camp. They said he was "dangerous," and it turned out they were right. But I never thought he was a hero. To a journalist, such a character is neither good nor bad, only interesting. And what was primarily interesting about this man was the fact that in 1983 he had gone off into what remains a pretty awesome wilderness, and he had stayed for a year.

Near the center of this great Gila wilderness, in a cave a few miles downstream from where Sapillo Creek meets the main branch of the Gila River in northern Grant County, Martin Price made his new home in

Martin Price, the "Gila Monster." Illustration by M. F. Barraza.
Courtesy of M. F. Barraza.

June of 1983. He brought with him a subsistence lifestyle and the myth of the mountain man.

"The Gila is the Yellowstone of the Southwest," Price told me. "I loved it. It was my home, but it brought me to this cage."

This day, Martin Price, thirty-one, was a resident of the Grant County Jail. Nearly a year after he moved into that cave at Panther Canyon, he was arrested by officers on horseback and charged with twenty-three counts of cattle rustling, burglary, littering, and poaching of wild game. In November 1984, he pleaded guilty to one count of each charge and received a two-year deferred sentence, a condition that included a nine-month jail term. He had served most of that nine-month term while awaiting sentencing and was eligible for release on probation in January 1985.

"I've got a ranch job lined up in Arizona," Price said. "It'll be legit and I can still live in the hills. I hope to live a lot like I always did, only I won't be killing cows anymore."

Long before his stay in the Gila Wilderness, Price chose to live in the woods, always picking mountainous terrain in the West.

"I lived for seven years mostly in the wilds. I lived for months at a time in the Chiricahua Mountains, in the Santa Catalina Mountains and the Mazatzal Wilderness, all in Arizona. Also, in central Nevada and in the Sawtooth Mountains in Idaho. In the Sawtooth Mountains I had a dog, a German shepherd pup, for company . . . until he was killed by a bear."

Price was not born into a remote rural lifestyle. His upbringing was in Arizona, for the most part, and at times in Sonora, Mexico, always in an unremarkable middle-class home. His father was in the mining business.

"It didn't matter where I was, I was always out in the desert or in the hills. That's what I liked. And when I got some schooling, I began to read Indian stories and all about mountain men. When I was four or five, my dad was at the silver mine in Puerto Libertad in Sonora. It was there that I first became friends with lizards. People laugh, but I can communicate with lizards; they're my friends. That's how I got the name 'Gila Monster.'"

Price was born with an affinity for the outdoors, but had no more of the skills needed to live there than any other middle-class person.

He acquired some of those skills in the military—three years as a paratrooper in the 82nd Airborne.

"I had a very difficult time in the military. I liked the soldiering; I liked guns and learned about weapons. I didn't like the discipline."

What Price learned about guns in the military he would put to use in later years in the wilderness.

"When I first went to the woods, I survived mostly by hunting. In the Gila I hunted squirrels—tassel-eared squirrels, rock squirrels, and Arizona grays. Turkey and deer—I'm learning how to work hides. Not many rabbits in that part of the Gila, but plenty of fish. I caught suckers, catfish, and trout. I speared them and I made fish traps. I caught bullfrogs."

Price said he was learning how to use homemade traps and a bow, but he did most of his hunting with guns. At his Gila camp he had a .22 rifle, a .270 rifle, and a .41 Magnum revolver, all with open sights.

"I didn't want a scope," Price said. "I wanted to get close."

One of the creatures Price got close to in the wilderness and leveled on with his iron gunsight was a domestic animal.

"Yes," he admitted, "I also hunted cows."

And, with that, Price's life in the wilderness came up against the law. Price did not equivocate.

"I couldn't live out there without breaking the law. For one thing, it's against the law nowadays to live in the wilderness. You can only stay so long and you're supposed to get out."

And hunting today, as Price found out, is not what it was when the mountain men roamed the Gila. The game is there, but it's protected by a bureaucracy and rules to match any found in urban life. You can kill a deer, but only at a certain time and in a certain way, and you're supposed to have a license. The squirrel season is two months long. The bullfrog season is shorter than that. And it is not legal to spear game fish.

"It's against the law to live off the land anymore," Price lamented.

One would expect a tirade here, a protest of the U.S. Forest Service, the New Mexico Game and Fish Department, et al. But it doesn't come.

"Basically, I think those guys are doing a damn good job," Price said. "The Gila Wilderness is special. I'm glad they could save some of it. Those guys like the wilderness too."

In Silver City, after Price was arrested, many people belittled his living off the land because he had poached game and rustled cattle. Price said, "I went six months at one point without seeing another person. That's something. I am a student of *son-hak*, the art of being a hermit. I worked in the wilderness to develop my mental powers to be a hermit. In time, it felt natural to live alone. Of course, I wasn't alone, really. I can communicate with animals. I was not alone at all. And I didn't kill animals in the area where I lived. I only killed what I actually needed. I suffered remorse at times after wounding and having to kill with my bare hands. I was an animal too. But then, we are all animals."

Price did not think he had any more natural ability for living outdoors than any other person, merely more of a liking for it. He did believe he developed outdoor skills during seven years in the wilds.

"Your senses develop in the wilderness. I concentrated on a different sense each day—hearing, sight, smell. I'd trail an animal and smell his track. Every human being has that ability to develop these senses . . . we have been dulled by modern society."

Price talked at length about his campsite. "I have always been a backpacker, never used horses or burros. I packed in four loads on my back. My cave was about a mile up Panther Canyon from the [Gila] river, up above the canyon, where I could see all around. But I was totally concealed from the river. I had a couple of sleeping bags and army blankets. I packed in tea and sugar and salt . . . some food. But, soon, I had nothing but what I could get myself. My camp was in the zone of pine and piñon and oak and manzanita. I learned to make use of six kinds of plants. I had started a garden when they caught me. That garden was a rock garden . . . I had to clear it. I had three bald eagles near camp. They stayed up by where the Sapillo comes in. But one would fly up and down the river every day, right by camp. And in the cave I slept by the fire, and I could lay on my back and see the fire and the stars.

"It was cold that winter, though it was really a mild winter for the Gila. But it was very cold. At first, I was all bundled up. But there I was on a January morning standing at the mouth of my cave in a T-shirt and bare feet.

"I'd cross the river in winter and I'd just take my clothes off and cross in my bare feet. When they came to arrest me, all the officers had jackets on, and I was barefoot already that spring. Their mouths dropped open when they saw how I was dressed in the cold. There was a good snow one night, but I just brushed it out of the cave in the morning.

That snow was less than the one in Idaho, in the Sawtooth Mountains in June. I was snowed in for two days there. I ran out of wood and had no fire. I ate elk meat raw, and that warmed me up. I felt healthy in the wilderness. I was healthy. I was never sick in the Gila. I've been sick several times in here."

What about Ben Lilly, last of the mountain men, who lived for long periods of time in the Gila, alone with his hounds as a government hunter, killing bear and lion for bounty?

"I've heard about him. I'd like to read his book, *The Ben Lilly Legend*. But Ben Lilly wouldn't be allowed to live like that today, any more than me."

And what of society, which cut short your life in the Gila and put you in a cage?

"True individuals are a rare species today. There's no room for an individual anymore. Not just in the wilderness, but anywhere. Our society won't allow it."

Price said he was a religious man. As he described his beliefs, I was reminded of the nineteenth-century New England transcendentalists whom, with the exception of Henry David Thoreau, Price had not read.

"I've read Thoreau, but I'm not that educated. I don't read or write that good. But I believe in the Great Spirit, what most people call God. I see God in the trees, plants, rocks. It's all connected. Trees, rocks, water—it's all connected and perfect the way it is, the way it operates. I learned all that in the wilderness. But I've learned some things in here too. When I was brought to the cage, people were talking like I was dangerous and didn't like people. I like being alone, but I don't dislike people. And in here, I'm starting to reestablish human relationships. I've made some good friends in here. And I'm getting to know my parents again. When I first came to this cage, I had culture shock. Getting used to people was the hard part. But I don't think I'd want to go back to being so alone anymore."

Price seemed to have a particular fondness for the television set.

"I'm missing my afternoon's TV with this interview. After a year without any TV, I've spent a lot of time with it in here. I've learned from TV too. I watch the performers and the people in the news and the politicians and I see who has succeeded. It's the people who are positive about life. It's the doers. I learned that was true in the wilderness, and now I see it here, on television. I think we are destined by fate. But I believe you can alter your destiny. You go to the wilderness and you don't know if you can do it. You face a crisis every day and you get scared. You find out that you can do it, and you become more positive about life. You learn to stay calm. I learned to be self-reliant—I like to be self-reliant—and that makes me believe in myself. I believe in myself."

Martin Price did not talk only about his time in the Gila and in the Grant County jail. Some questions took him back to other places where he'd lived in the woods, when he wasn't always by himself.

"I had that dog in the Sawtooth Mountains. That was company, for a while. And for a while in the woods, this guy camped with me. He didn't last. I lived with a girl too, and she didn't last. I burned up three times the wood when she was there. She married fire. She was afraid to leave the fire. Some women like the idea of living in the wilderness, but they change when they get there. They don't like the reality. And then, I lived with Susan and her four kids. Those were the best days, with Susan and those kids. Then she left the wilderness. When she was gone, I didn't want to be with nobody anymore. I felt hurt and hostility. That's when I came to the Gila to live alone. I've gotten over most of the hurt and hostility now, living in the Gila and being in here too. And since she left, I've been celibate. I've been celibate for two and a half years. I will end that soon, as soon as I get out of here. But that was the best—when I lived in the wilderness with Susan and those kids. You come into camp at night and a woman and kids are there, and they have the fire ready and you've got a deer slung over your shoulder. That was it. And a lot of people have told me that they would like to live like I did, if they could. They can't. I can't. Not anymore. I've learned my lesson. I was born one hundred years too late."

After his release from the Grant County jail Martin Price went back to Arizona, but he didn't take that ranch job. He kept disappearing into the wilderness, then, following another capture, he would spend time in jail. For a time I corresponded with him. He said of all the wilderness he knew, the Gila was his favorite, "the Yellowstone of the Southwest." He regretted he couldn't go back there. "I'm too well known," he said. But his letters were tinged with threats against anyone who would impinge on his lifestyle. There was increasingly less romance and more venom and pathology in the letters and lifestyle of Martin Price. Then I lost touch.

About ten years after his time spent in the Gila, he disappeared into the mountains for the last time, near Prescott, Arizona. Soon, area ranchers began losing cattle, and there was evidence of deer and javelina poaching in the region. Sheriff's deputies went into the mountains to arrest him. One day, years later, another who had an interest in Martin Price came by my bookshop; he wanted to talk about the "Gila Monster." He had a book in mind and wanted to know what I knew of the man. I knew plenty, and shared my thoughts, but I did not know the details of how Martin Price went down. This man was a psychologist and had counseled the deputy who ended the life of Martin Price, a common practice in modern law enforcement whenever an officer uses deadly force. He told it like this.

"The two Yavapai County deputies went looking for him. They found his camp, but Price had slipped out ahead. They split up and trailed him, one taking the flank. But Price doubled back and got the drop on the lead deputy. He had him on his knees at gunpoint when the second deputy, on the flank, came over a rise and saw the standoff; his partner was disarmed and Price's rifle was pointed at his chest. The deputy aimed and fired, missing Price but hitting the stock of his rifle. The bullet ricocheted off the rifle stock and by chance struck Price in the heart."

This was not Ben Lilly bidding a peaceful if foggy farewell to the wild waters and far mountains. The Gila Monster was dead, holding a violent grip on a lifestyle that had passed him by, an odd and certainly imperfect end to the western myth and the Gila's legacy of mountain men and other characters.

Aldo Leopold, hunter, fly-fisher, conservationist. Courtesy of
New Mexico Wildlife Federation.

The Origins of the
Wilderness Ethic

BY THE EARLY 1900S HUNTER TOM WOOD, BEN LILLY, AND A HOST OF other wilderness nimrods, homesteaders, and survivalists had already done a good share of their work. In the absence, or poor enforcement, of game laws, game animals declined markedly. In *Recollections of a Western Ranchman* Captain William French described a single extended hunt, in an autumn week in the 1880s, that included Navajo Indians hunting with several area ranchers between the San Francisco and Blue rivers. Such was the devastating lust to get the meat, get the deer, and get them all in this single, organized hunt that the deer herd in the region, French said, never recovered. French participated in the hunt but lamented the "wanton destruction" of more than eighty animals, an act that displayed no concept of limits, sustainability, or the future.

In an 1880s fishing trip into the headwaters of the Gila, French marveled at the beautiful "speckled trout"; they were delicious and readily caught. He could not know that these were the native Gila trout of the Gila drainage, a species unto themselves, rare by their very isolation, though at that time locally numerous. Within twenty years of stocking rainbow trout, officially and unofficially, the species was threatened with genetic obsolescence through interbreeding.

On the same fishing trip French saw a small herd of native Gila elk, the so-called Merriam's subspecies. To my knowledge he was the last to chronicle the animal by sight; within a few years the subspecies was

extinct, the elk no longer a resident of the Gila forest (in time new introductions from the northern Rockies would restore the species to the
region). And the pressure on wolves, bears, lions, and the jaguar (that
occasionally entered the Gila) was even more fierce; they were regarded
simply as noxious varmints. All their numbers shrank and the wolf,
grizzly, and jaguar were extirpated.

The Gila Wilderness itself was shrinking. Mule trails led to wagon
roads and soon motorized vehicles were making inroads into the wilderness. By this time the Gila watershed was no longer public domain open
to homesteaders like Tom Wood; its uplands at least, and much of the
lower drainage, was Forest Service land held and managed, in theory, for
production in perpetuity under Gifford Pinchot's philosophy of "highest and best use." This production did not include settlement, but it did
include logging, mining, grazing, and, with what was left, public recreation, including hunting, fishing, hiking, camping, and, as time passed,
industrialized tourism. As late as 1920 the idea that the "highest and
best use" might include a portion of forest left in its natural state was
still novel—even radical—in most official circles. Indeed, by then, "big
wilderness" was virtually gone in the Southwest; roads and vehicles had
virtually eliminated the wilds. A forester named Aldo Leopold thought
mightily of the concept of protecting wilderness within the scope of
entire landscapes. Where many land managers, under the Pinchot doctrine, saw wilderness as of low value, or no use at all, to Leopold such
lands and waters were "the perfect norm," the baseline prototype of what
constitutes a healthy forest. Having been a forester in the Southwest
for more than a dozen years, he knew he must act posthaste; he was
articulate and committed, and he penned his pleas and plans even as the
motor vehicle was taking the day and new roadways were being mapped
out for the lands he hoped to save.

In later years he wrote in "Wilderness and Its Place in Forest Recreation Policy" (*Journal of Forestry*, 1921), "In 1909, when I first moved
to the Southwest, there had been six blocks of roadless country, each
embracing half a million acres or more, in the national forests of Arizona
and New Mexico. By the 1920's new roads had invaded five of them and
there was only one left: the headwaters of the Gila River."

In the same article, he clearly defined a counterpoint, or at least an
adjunct, to Pinchot's "highest and best use."

"By wilderness," he wrote, "I mean a continuous stretch of country preserved in its natural state, open to lawful hunting and fishing, big enough to absorb a two weeks' pack trip, and kept devoid of roads, artificial trails, cottages, or other works of man."

Elsewhere in the article, he indicates he thought the Gila headwaters was not only the last place available, but arguably the best.

> The Southwest (meaning New Mexico and Arizona) is a distinct region. The original southwestern wilderness was the scene of several important chapters in our national history. The remainder of it is about as interesting from about as large a number of angles, as any place on the continent. It has a high and varied recreational value. Under the policy advocated in this paper, a good big sample of it should be preserved. This could easily be done by selecting such an area as the headwaters of the Gila River on the Gila National Forest. This is an area of nearly half a million acres [it would turn out to be nearly 800,000 acres], topographically isolated by mountain ranges and box canyons. It has not yet been penetrated by railroads and to only a very limited extent by roads. On account of the natural obstacles to transportation and the absence of any considerable areas of agricultural land, no net economic loss would result from the policy of withholding further industrial development . . . The entire region is the natural habitat of deer, elk, turkey, grouse, and trout. If preserved in its natural semi-virgin state, it could absorb a hundred pack trains each year without overcrowding. It is the last typical wilderness in the southwestern mountains. Highest use demands its preservation.

In 1925, in "A Plea for Wilderness Hunting Grounds" in *Outdoor Life*, Leopold further extolled the Gila's uniqueness. After again lamenting that within the Southwest all the other five big wilderness areas were gone, he wrote,

> Sixth, there was—and is—the headwaters of the Gila, in the Gila National Forest. The Creator must have foreseen the

present plight of the wilderness hunter, for in this precious
remnant of the old frontier he piled up the hills "high, wide,
and handsome." In every point where roads might enter is a
set of rugged mountains. Wherever a foaming trout stream
has cut its way thru the mountain wall a jagged box canyon
says, "They shall not pass" . . . This is the last stand—these
hills are meant to play in, not to stay in.

The same unique, improbable, and yet somehow fluid mix of perennial flows and forbidding mountains that had so inspired Mimbres
artists, Apache warriors, mountain men, and other characters had with-
stood, just long enough, the motor vehicle and its attendant roads. This
isolated natural area now grabbed the imagination of a forester who
articulated a wilderness management concept that would protect this
legacy of land and waters much as history had known it, possibly for all
time. In 1924, in response to Leopold's pleas, plans, and writings, the
U.S. Forest Service set aside nearly 800,000 acres of the Gila National
Forest, making it off limits to roads, vehicles, and "other works of man,"
yet open to camping, hiking, and "lawful hunting and fishing," as the
nation's first protected wilderness area. It was a "primitive" concept
that would grow in acreage and legitimacy thenceforth nationwide and
culminate in the Wilderness Act, passed by Congress and signed by
President Lyndon Johnson in 1964. Today our nation's wilderness system
totals more than 100 million acres. "An unlikely place for water" had
inspired an entire nation to take another look at how we should relate
to the natural world.

Ranching and Agriculture— Destruction or Sustainability?

THE WILDERNESS LABEL PROTECTED THE HEARTLAND OF THE GILA National Forest from roads and settlement, from source waters at Bead Spring at over 10,000 feet, to the confluence of Turkey Creek some 5,000 feet downstream—the headwaters of the Gila River. As stated, this was nearly 800,000 acres. Most of the Gila National Forest (it totals some 3.3 million acres in all) was thus *not* wilderness and management debates about the forest pervaded, as is inevitable. Overall, as the century proceeded, philosophical leanings and management changes were positive. Predators changed from varmints to game animals, to be targeted no more for elimination than the deer herd. Wolves have even been reintroduced, though not necessarily successfully; the return of the grizzly has been at least contemplated; and the river otter is scheduled for reintroduction. Fire was seen as always bad, then just sometimes bad, and is now seen as a natural process, a tool of ecosystem management; some wildfires must be put out, but others they start on purpose to thin the forest. It was a sometimes messy process, often contentious, but progress was made.

Nowhere was this progress more messy and contentious than the Gila's role in ranching and farming. Not even Aldo Leopold disapproved of either one, per se. Just as the Gila headwaters showed us the way in Wilderness, which left alone mostly sustains itself, the region can show us the way in agricultural sustainability, if we pick our prototypes with care. Following are three examples with which I have some personal familiarity of how the Gila's running waters provide us with lessons in agriculture, and some pondering for times to come.

Trouble on the Diamond Bar

About fifteen years ago I was invited to take a horseback ride with the Forest Service. With others representing agencies, the public, and the rancher himself, we were to look over a portion of the Diamond Bar Ranch, a roughly 200,000-acre grazing lease that drained the Diamond Creek complex, Black Canyon Creek, and other tributaries including a portion of the east fork of the Gila river. There was trouble coming and the Gila National Forest Service wanted input.

The Forest Service must take part of the blame from the get-go. They had signed a grazing permit lease with Kit Laney, et al., allowing more than one thousand cattle on the Diamond Bar. It was far too many cattle for the range, and worse, the cows quite naturally began to gather up and down the streams during the drier months, denuding the riparian habitats to the detriment of wildlife, especially the endangered Gila trout, which was supposedly being restored in the Diamond Creek complex, and later, Black Canyon. Within years these stream habitats, by general consensus, were "nuked." The Forest Service wanted us "enviros" to okay construction of dirt tanks with bulldozers in this portion of the wilderness to help draw the cows off the streams. The ride was fun, beautiful, and informative, and afterward at a line camp Laney and his wife, looking very much the part in full cowboy regalia, made impassioned pleas to "allow us to make a living off the land." I've always been taken by the lifeways of the traditional cowboy, make no apologies for it, and these two were the real thing. But none of us liked the look of the streams or the idea of bulldozers in a wilderness. I was conflicted. The official environmental response was: get rid of, or greatly reduce, the cows and restore the streams and that portion of the east fork on the Diamond Bar Ranch.

The battle raged for about fifteen years. The Forest Service sought to reduce, and further reduce, the allowable number of cattle; Laney resisted ("I've got a permit for 1,100 head!"), the enviros sued on behalf of the trout and other wildlife, and the stream habitats gradually went from bad to worse. A rancher I respect told me that with funding and man-power, they could have fenced off all streams and the east fork, allowed only "dormant season" grazing (roughly November through March), and made it work. Maybe so. But it would have been an enormous fencing job to complete and maintain, hardly cost effective, and was never seriously considered. In the end Laney claimed he didn't need a grazing permit because his grazing freedoms were a "property right" that preceded Forest Service authority over the Diamond Bar; *he* would decide what was the allowable number of cattle on the ranch, and though he never backed it up, even claimed he could keep the public—he told this eye-to-eye to a fishing buddy of mine—off the land, though it was all but 120 acres part of the Gila National Forest.

In the end, in my view, nobody looked very good. But the courts mercifully ended it. They said a grazing lease is *not* a property right and backed up the Forest Service when they finally yanked the grazing permit and organized the roundup of the cattle. Laney fought the removal of the cattle; the courts backed the Forest Service again. At one point there was an altercation on horseback; Laney did time, and I last heard he said he was headed for Argentina to start over as a cattleman. As of this writing the Diamond Bar is essentially "cow free" and that portion of the east fork and its tributaries—Diamond Creek and Black Canyon—are making a remarkable recovery as riparian zones. The trout are doing better too. But it was a terribly rough lesson about carrying capacity and sustainability of lands and waters.

A Place for Cows and Birds

A ranch with a far different lesson is the U-Bar, perhaps fifty miles downstream along the Gila River near Cliff, New Mexico, and owned by Freeport-McMoran Inc. Granted, it is not comparable with the Diamond Bar. The U-Bar is far smaller, on private lands, and more readily available to intensive management. But it offers the same potential conflict between cows, a river, riparian habitats, and wildlife. Yet here the conflicts have been handled far differently. My son Bud and I went there early one morning to see if it might offer a different lesson in how to relate livestock, and people, with the natural world. Arriving at the river bridge at 6 a.m. to meet the others, I commented that I had been up this early before to hunt birds, but never just to watch them. Was I acting smart or just admitting that I had something to learn? Maybe a little of both.

Our search was not for the usual count of bird species—though we would take note of every different bird we saw—but instead for one rather small, drab brown bird in particular. The willow flycatcher, an unobtrusive little flit in the trees, is nonetheless the center of much controversy. This flycatcher is on the list of federally endangered species, with all that implies. The bird knows nothing of this, of course, but since the listing the creature has inspired or angered a host of folks who otherwise wouldn't know it existed. The few flycatchers that are left live in select riparian areas in the Southwest. Most riparian areas in the Southwest have been greatly depleted and, sure enough, our guide Scott Stoleson would tell us that it is destruction or alteration of habitat, by cows, dams, urban growth, channelization, and dewatering, that is behind the decline in willow flycatcher numbers. We ducked under the fence into a pasture of the U-Bar and started up the river. The bird watchers among us picked out the call of the yellow warbler right away. Then a pair of night herons flew over. A pair of mallard ducks came up off the water. And in under the trees we saw the first of several willow flycatchers. A furtive little thing, none let us have a look for long before they flew back into the riparian canopy and disappeared. And according to Stoleson, they are pretty tough too.

The cowbird has a parasitic relationship with some species in riparian habitats—they take over the nests of weaker birds and thereby ruin the reproduction of their hosts. They "run" with cows and they are implicated in the decline of the willow flycatcher; they thereby also implicate the cow. But Stoleson said it's not that simple.

"The willow flycatcher will often fight them off," Stoleson said. "I've seen them fly at the cowbirds, and you could hear them thumping the cowbirds on the back."

It was a lovely riparian swath along the Gila River—lots of big cottonwoods, some of them over a hundred feet tall, sycamores, box elders, and willows. Oddly, it is box elder more than willow that is indicative of willow flycatcher habitat.

"Really, they don't particularly like willow," Stoleson said.

Our guide told us that this area along the Gila "has the highest density of noncolonial breeding birds in North America." He also explained this was due to the habitat having a rare combination of benefits, including an interphase between subtropical and temperate zones, sun, a perennial, free-flowing river; and warmth, which encourages a lot of vegetative productivity and variety, both old growth and new growth, and a tall canopy. The pasture we were in had not been grazed by livestock in ten years. Livestock grazing is a commonly named culprit in riparian habitat loss in the Southwest, yet Stoleson pointed across a field to another stringer of riparian growth that he said is grazed periodically, though not continually, throughout the year.

"The flycatcher does quite well there," he said.

We left this pasture and drove downstream to another, this one a section (about 640 acres) of land that is grazed November to March (dormant season grazing) by about 150 cows. Where the previous pasture has proven to be good flycatcher habitat, this was even better.

"Right now there are about forty nesting pairs [of flycatchers] in this pasture," ranch manager David Ogilvie said, "the highest known anywhere."

As we moved into the trees, it was easy to surmise why. Both the understory of vegetation and the canopy were thicker. The habitat was enhanced, we were told, not only by proximity to the river, but also by subirrigation, some of it natural, some of it coming via runoff from adjacent farmlands. I got a good look at a willow flycatcher nest, a cone-shaped little construction that momentarily sported one of the parent birds before he, typically, disappeared before our eyes.

By now Bud was bored and was becoming a pest, about right for a six-year-old who had to get up at 5 a.m. Fortunately, we adjourned to the river's edge where he regained focus watching tadpoles swimming, bullfrogs hopping, and a big carp nosing around on the bottom. The river habitats were lush and good; dormant season grazing seemed to work along the river too. The highlight at the water for all of us was a Bullock's oriole, such a bright orange and yellow bird you could spot him sitting in a tree clear across the river. Then he took flight, came to us, and flashed his colors as he went by.

There were enviros in our group, and agency people, as well as our guide, and the rancher who managed the cows, and a bird hunter-journalist and his kid. There was not, however, anyone to utter a discouraging word; nobody to slam the grazing of cows in riparian areas, a big issue wherever people and cows compete for the rare benefits of running water in the great Southwest. Having been around the argument for a while, I think I can take that part.

Willow flycatchers don't need cows, the critic would say; the bird was here in abundance for ages before anyone thought to graze domestic livestock along streams. As we eliminate grazing from riparian areas, the depleted habitats will be restored and flycatchers and other fauna will return to replicate the ancient norm. That ancient norm did not include cows. Maybe so. But it's hard to argue with success. Forty breeding pairs in one 640-acre pasture is a rich abundance of an otherwise rare bird. Clearly, bad grazing continues to deplete riparian habitats. And clearly, managed grazing, as it's done on the U-Bar Ranch along the Gila, is compatible with willow flycatchers and lush habitats and may even help the critter in ways we do not yet understand. What scares me is not cows, but the future—how do we hold on to open spaces, whether wild lands, or wild, free-flowing rivers, or the rural, pastoral, agricultural ambience, in the face of surging human population? The norm today is growth, the conversion of open spaces and scarce water to the "highest and best use"—usually meaning another subdivision—an urban criteria driven by unmitigated profit that spells defeat for rancher, enviro, bird hunter, and bird watcher alike. I'll work with anyone, whether or not he has cows or a tractor, who will help stem the tide.

On the way out we saw a Mexican black hawk sitting on a tree. It's a large predator, impressive in flight or even at rest. Like the colorful Bullock's oriole, it is easy to defend. The small, drab willow flycatcher is not so easy to defend. That there are such a variety of people willing to defend it, and its habitat, was the best sign I saw all day.

"Sure was a good bird watch," Bud said as we drove away.

"Yes," I said, "there's hope."

Bettering the Ancient Ones

Earlier in the book I described the rise, flourishing, decline, and disappearance of the ancient Mogollon culture along the Gila and Mimbres rivers. Through farming they developed for a time a successful agriculture that allowed for a century or two of some leisure time, which prompted a handful of remarkable artists to flourish and create images we still marvel at today. Their agriculture was often the subject of their art. Yet in the end they had not the knowledge or the means to make their lands better; as the lands declined in health and productivity, the culture in time was forced into desperation and they abandoned the valleys. Well, despite the USDA, agribusiness, and PhDs in agronomy, most modern farmers don't know how to better the land while taking from it either. But at the No Cattle Company in the Mimbres Valley, in the shadow of an ancient culture, I found an example of intensive agriculture that nonetheless produces sustainably.

In agribusiness, monoculture is the word. If you're a pecan farmer, you haven't the time or know-how to fool around with chiles, or visaversa. All farmers specialize now, it is said, and the trend is led, or at least reinforced, by the ag schools. But at the No Cattle Company, up along the Mimbres River, it's agri*culture*, not agri*business*, and you need to know everything from green apples to green manure.

"Monoculture doesn't do it here," says Sharlene Grunerud. Her partner, Michael Alexander, adds, "Diversification is the key to our success. You can lose a crop in any year, but we always have others to carry us through."

Grunerud and Alexander are the managers, workers, and shareholders of the forty-three-acre parcel, about thirteen acres of which is irrigated farmland, with about nine acres of that in orchard and nearly four acres in vegetables and flowers. I couldn't write fast enough to get it all down, but here is some of the produce you could spread your table with from this farm: pinto beans; radishes; tomatoes; a host of shrubs, vines, and small trees (most of which are grown from cuttings); a variety of flowers; apples (red delicious, Jonathan, golden delicious, among others); pears; onions; winter squash; eggplant; herbs; summer squash; chiles (five varieties); Swiss chard; lettuce; collard greens; kale; rhubarb; corn; and clover, oats, and winter wheat (grown as green manure). Clearly one needs knowledge, not only of crop production, but also of crop relationships, to make this small farm go. And it's all organic.

"Organic certification is a marketing tool for us," Alexander says. "We wouldn't use chemicals in any event."

And organic can be a tricky business. The Organic Food Production Act, passed by Congress in 1990 and since updated by USDA regulations, set standards for organic produce. Also in 1990, the New

Mexico legislature established the New Mexico Organic Commodity Commission (NMOCC). Its five commissioners certify organic growers within the state.

"Basically, the Feds certify the certifiers," Alexander says.

The end result, according to the NMOCC, is that consumers can know that the organic foods they buy are "rich in nutrients and free of chemical-based fertilizers, herbicides and pesticides."

What it means to the No Cattle Company is record keeping.

"We have to record all the details, every time we plant and every time we harvest," Alexander says.

Grunerud says, "Our vegetable business is a seed to market operation. We grow our own transplants from both saved seed and purchased seed." Essentially that means they take their crops from start to finish, with some of the crops started in one of two greenhouses, and the finish being sale either at the wholesale market or retail at the farmers' market in Silver City.

"The Saturday market [in Silver City] is real important to us," Grunerud says. "Though at a market like Santa Fe, we could get twice as much for the same crop."

This is a production farm, not a hobby farm; nonetheless the ambiance is positively bucolic. A diversion of the Mimbres River runs through the land. Trees surround the farm plots—some small plots, the biggest at four acres. The farm lists bobcat, deer, elk, ringtail cat, javelina, fox, squirrels, raccoon, rabbits, porcupine, coatimundi, and skunks as common residents or visitors. Not to mention a myriad of bird life that is attracted to any riparian area in the desert, trout in the stream, and the occasional family of bears.

"In 1994," they tell me, "three black bears called the farm home for about four months. They slept in the cottonwood trees during the day, coming out at night to clean up the windfall fruit. They were well-behaved bears and left when the apples were gone."

An argument for the diverse farm versus the monocultural farm has always been the ancillary benefit of wildlife and habitat. This is easily seen at the No Cattle Company. Pests can be devilish on any farm, especially when you can't spray pesticides. Grunerud and Alexander use a variety of means to control pests, from picking squash bugs by hand, to trapping pocket gophers, to cultivating bats.

"Codling moth is our number one pest in the orchards," Alexander says. "The most promising [control] in our opinion is bats. We have several bat houses around the farm. Bats also control cucumber beetles, mosquitoes, corn earworm, and a variety of others pests."

Any farm will live or die by the quality of the soil. We walk to the four-acre plot and I am told the organic matter in the field was tested at 2.5 percent.

"That's good for this desert environment," Alexander says.

And the tillage has been excellent. I watch as Alexander takes a four-foot rod and pokes it down into the dirt, right up to the hilt.

"With a moldboard plow you can develop a hardpan just under the surface," Alexander says. "We use a subsoiler."

This implement is new to me. We take a look and it is basically a rotating cultivator that digs real deep. That deep tillage turns in the green manure and compost and maintains fertile, arable soil. The soil on this four-acre plot is richer than the natural soil that surrounds it, and richer than when they began farming it. That's sustainability *plus*.

Grunerud says, "John is our third partner; that is, John Deere."

At the No Cattle Company they have a 72-horsepower John Deere tractor. It pulls the subsoiler and a rolling cultivator that weeds between the rows, and they run a thrashing machine and cider press off the PTO (power takeoff). Still, there is plenty of hand labor.

"There is still a lot of weeding with a hoe between the plants," Grunerud says.

That kind of work and the long hours inherent in farming are the sober, practical side of making it on the land. Going back to Thomas Jefferson and Henry David Thoreau, it has always been the American ideal—the yeoman farmer.

"There's ways of doing it," Grunerud says, "but you have to be able to fix the tractor."

And most everything else, it seems.

"If you have to hire someone to make or fix all the things you need, you'll never make it," she adds.

Fortunately Grunerud and Alexander, in particular, have good mechanical skills.

"He's my renaissance man," she says.

Along with diversification, renaissance may be the word for this entire farm. At the Wisconsin State Fair in 1859, Abraham Lincoln gave a speech: "The greatest fine art of the future," he said, "will be the making of a comfortable living from a small piece of land." At the No Cattle Company, Lincoln's vision of agriculture still resonates well, even in a modern world of monoculture and agribusiness. Were such an agricultural ethic to catch on, it could, as along the Mimbres a thousand years ago, produce a nation, or at least a subculture, of artists.

Today, up and down the Mimbres Valley, acres of farmland and the natural world have been lost to subdivision. But here on forty-three acres is a parcel the ancient Mimbres would have recognized, especially from their better years. One can only surmise that they would have marveled at this oasis of productivity the river has provided—and would have approved. Had they known as much, perhaps they could have stayed on.

The gamest fish that swims inhabits the Gila's waters. Photo by Jan Haley.

SEVEN

Fish Stories, Bird Tales,
River Runs, and Recreation

RECREATION IS A PRICELESS, GOLDEN WORD THAT HAS LARGELY LOST ITS meaning through overuse, commonality, an ignorance of its etymology, and general defeat in the political arena by more "serious" verbiage like *markets, profits, cost/benefits, jobs, growth,* and *bottom line.* I'll have something to say myself about cost/benefits in the next chapter. But the fight over the Gila River's future in New Mexico boils down to people and their values. Mining, logging, grazing, and the diversion of water to promote growth still have their place along the river, but, as we've seen, people also care about isolated wild trout few have ever seen and "worthless" misnamed flycatchers. Growth and commerce are often undeniably at odds with such amenities, and, at least within the realm of western states water management, have almost always held sway. Yet, with a proper respect for *re-creation,* the Gila River's singular past could yield to a future like none other in the Southwest. For so many of us—including some who have only known the river by reputation, readings, or word of mouth—recreation along the Gila is more than mere diversion, and more than a draw for tourism dollars. It's *restorative,* to land, water, wildlife, and humankind alike, and literally more than money can buy. Nothing speaks more directly to the Gila's riparian powers of restoration than its peculiar mix of fish and birds. For me, all this is best told from personal experience, what I've known from my own time along the river. So here are some fish stories, and a couple more bird tales.

Natives, Non-natives, and Exotics

When James Ohio Pattie first encountered the Gila River in 1825, he commented that it was clear and swift, rocky, about thirty yards wide, and "filled with fish." He doesn't name the fish but says they cooked them in the hot springs at a fork in the river. It appears that his party arrived at a mountainous portion of the Gila, above today's Cliff-Gila Valley and perhaps around the Sapillo Creek confluence. He says they went upstream to the forks, implying it took several days. The Gila's fishery was much less diverse then than now, and since these fish were eating size, they must have been either Gila trout, roundtail chub, desert sucker, or Sonora sucker. My romantic inclination says they were Gila trout; they certainly would have been the best eating of the lot, the others being rather boney.

When William Emory arrived at the Gila in 1846, it was still a natural river. Emory quite clearly states they saw the Gila at the mouth of what is now Mangas Creek; he added the fish were so numerous you could "hear them playing in the waters." He describes them as an unknown species that were much like trout "but then I saw the difference." Emory was too far downstream for the Gila trout, which needs cooler mountain waters, and had encountered the roundtail chub. He says they were edible with the flesh "soft and more like catfish than trout."

Other fish, minnows or minnow-sized, inhabited the presettlement Gila, but the angler will quickly note that the historic Gila in New Mexico held exactly one fish a fisherman today would call a game fish—the Gila trout—and it only inhabited the colder waters of the drainage. Today that has changed. By hook, crook, or legal introduction, the following are now all found in the Gila drainage in places between the source springs and the Arizona state line: Gila trout, rainbow trout, rainbow/Gila hybrids, rainbow/cutthroat hybrids, brook trout (in Whitewater Creek), brown trout, channel catfish, flathead catfish, smallmouth bass, largemouth bass, bluegill, bullheads, sunfish, and carp. Even counting the carp and bullheads as "rough" fish, the Gila's game fish are now more diverse, and inhabit more water than the historic norm by about ten to one.

Yet I have heard biologists at times refer to the Gila as a "collapsed fishery." This is understandable. Some of the natives, like the Gila trout, spike dace, and loach minnow are threatened or endangered, while some of those species that nature didn't put there, like bass and catfish, flourish. The biologist naturally laments the declining endemic minnow; the

Bud Salmon with a thirty-inch "exotic" carp. Courtesy of M. H. Salmon.

angler exalts at the twenty-inch wild brown he just caught that was born and raised in the stream, even if its ancestry traces from elsewhere. Has this fishery collapsed or been rejuvenated?

There can be no denying that native species, non-native species, and exotic species are sometimes in conflict with one another, and with man. Because of the conflict, we must at times favor a given species to help it survive the competition. But this bias may place another species in disfavor, or even in jeopardy. The critter I like may be the one you'd just as soon be rid of. "Natives, non-natives, and exotics" is a can of worms, but it contains an important issue and we need to open this can before we fish the Gila drainage.

A native species is one that has occurred naturally in a given area over time. For example, the channel catfish and flathead catfish have lived in the Rio Grande in New Mexico for untold millennia; they were here before the Indians, and the first European settlers found them and caught them in the "great river" before we humans turned it into an often dewatered canal.

Less than a hundred miles from the Rio Grande, west of the Continental Divide, is the upper Gila River. Historically, it had no catfish. But now channel cats and flatheads have been introduced and are self-sustaining in that water. The channel cat and flathead are thus "native" to the Rio Grande but "non-native" to the Gila drainage just a short distance away.

An "exotic" species is one that exists even further afield, as on another continent, or at least in another country. Prominent exotics in America include the brown trout (from Scotland and Germany), the ring-necked pheasant (from China), and the red fox (from England). The red fox in particular fools people. It seems as if it's a native, as it has been here for centuries, is wide-ranging, and is a fixture of American fauna and culture. But there were no red fox in the Lower 48 until George Washington and other hunters in the colonial period had them brought over from the United Kingdom because they gave a better race for the hounds than the native gray fox.

Time was when the introduction of non-natives and exotics was quite the rage; that's how so many catfish, brown trout, pheasants, and red fox got in so many places where nature didn't put them. Many of these introductions received general approval at the time—and do so today—for these are enticing game animals that have found a niche and provide great sport, pleasure, food, fur, and sometimes profit. If they at times dominate, or extirpate, some of the natives, it has still been seen as more gain than loss.

But times change. Some exotics, like the brown rat, starling, and in places the carp, have clearly been mostly trouble. And most people, including virtually all wildlife professionals, now think that natives are the preferred wildlife in their habitats and should not be pushed out by non-natives or exotics. Within limits, I'm of this view myself.

Favoring and restoring natives opens its own can of worms, however, for to bring the natives back you may have to extirpate the interlopers, some of whom, like the red fox, brown trout, and pheasant have become part of the local fauna and culture, and folks aren't about to give them up. This issue is evident in a look at the native, non-native, and exotic fish of the Gila drainage in New Mexico. So let's briefly open this can of worms, looking at the federally endangered Gila trout and the state endangered roundtail chub. Should we save them? *Can* we save them? Regarding their non-native and exotic competitors, to what extreme are we willing to go to try to gut the competition?

To date, and counting the upper west fork of the Gila, the Gila trout has been restored to nearly one hundred miles of Gila water, entirely high country streams. It has recently been downlisted from endangered to threatened, which could allow for some catch-and-release fishing. The main impediment has been that Gila trout hybridize with the introduced rainbows and, by today's state and federal wildlife agency standards, must be 100 percent pure by genetic analysis "to contribute to recovery of species." This standard has led to the poisoning of streams, killing trout en masse that are more than 90 percent pure and look, breed, and behave for all the world like Gila trout. Some streams have been poisoned and restocked several times, and the elusive 100 percent purity standard is still not met, with more poisoning being planned. To me, the goal of restoration is laudable, the methods at times extreme. In stream surveys, state and federal biologists regularly "bank" any non-native fish they net or electro-fish to the surface. This means they gut and toss up on the bank anything they think doesn't belong there. This could be a twenty-inch brown that would be a trophy to enjoy and release for an angler, but an "exotic" with a suspect ancestry for a biologist.

Some suggestions: Stop stocking rainbows in the Gila drainage (incredibly, the New Mexico Department of Game and Fish still does this); genetically "swamp" with stockings of Gila trout; poison streams, or electro-fish, selectively only when the genetic analysis falls below 90 to 95 percent; make the 100 percent purity standard a goal, not an untouchable requirement; don't worry about the browns. Wild rainbows compete favorably with browns in many Gila streams and throughout the West, and the Gila trout should too; you can always liberalize the "take" on browns. Finally, whenever possible, stock with wild Gila trout; they're better than the stockers even if they lack a degree or two of purity.

The roundtail chub favors warmer waters than the Gila trout and competes with bass, trout, catfish, carp, and perhaps other predators, like crawfish, which are not native to the Gila but are here to stay. The chub appear to be holding out fairly well in the west, middle, and particularly the east forks of the Gila, but are scarce or gone from the main stem below the forks. The attempted forced removal of smallmouth bass, channel cat, flathead catfish, and carp from the main Gila is preposterous, though some biologists would love to give it a try. You'd spend a fortune in the effort, and you'd never get them all, but done year by year you could get enough to ruin the sport fishery. Imagine the public ire as biologists throw a four-pound bronze bass or twenty-pound flathead catfish up on the bank, all for the roundtail chub!

There is a twenty-mile stretch of the west fork below Gila trout territory and above the Gila Cliff Dwellings. It's not great bass water, but you could electro-fish and remove those few bass that live over that stretch. Leave all the trout, native or non-native; the chub evolved with trout, so they should be able to compete with trout. There are virtually no carp or catfish in this reach. There is already a breeding population of chub there; this could be a wild "hatchery" for stocking in other reaches. On the main Gila, liberalize the take of small bass and release the trophies. This could make lunker wilderness bass a trophy fish and help the chub at the same time.

These are just some preliminary thoughts to show that we can find ways to help the natives without starting a foolishly draconian war against newer arrivals who have over the past hundred years established their own values in the drainage. In the future will we be fishing for one game species or for ten? Can we restore a native without eliminating diversity? Is there value to that diversity, even if some of it is man-made? In the nation's first wilderness, within the state's last free flow, each species offers its own appeal along the waters. Let's wet a line and see what we come up with.

Fishing: A Personal Response to Madness

It was my first outing since a few of those people killed so many of our people at the World Trade Center and the Pentagon. I'd say terrorists but overuse has rendered the word too mild for the likes of them, and the word I have in mind won't do with the tone of this volume. But it was the world gone mad, and we all got a good look at the crazed in action on the morning and evening news, over and over again.

From the president on down I began to hear that, although our world had changed, we Americans must get back to the business of the nation and try to live our lives much as before. Shake it off, clear your head, and get on with it. I would later come to dispute much of George Bush's response to the "war on terror," but his call for us to get on with it hit home; lose your spirit, take flight from your life, and they have already won.

For me, "clear your head" means you grab a fishing rod and head for a stretch of running water where with luck you won't see anybody all day. We still have such places in southwest New Mexico, especially if you go on a weekday and get an early start. I left the truck at the end of the road and began a hike downstream. This was a river reach of the Gila where channel catfish, flathead catfish, and smallmouth bass were all possible, along with suckers and carp. I had a fly rod in my hand and a mix of artificial flies in my vest. Catfish, carp, and suckers are rarely caught on artificial flies, so I was hoping for a bronze bass. I found the river running fast and high and murky. Maybe too murky for a bass to flash to a fly, but I was in it for the day and was going to fish regardless. A large fly was in order, so the fish could see it. I tied on a muddler minnow, a big furry-looking thing wound on a #8 hook. I cast and drifted it through a variety of habitats as I worked my way downstream. I couldn't draw a hit in pool, riffle, or run, so I switched to a Pistol Pete, thinking the bright buzz of the propeller might draw a strike in a cloudy stream. I cast that one until a lack of success and the slant of the sun told me it was time to break for lunch.

I had a great view of the world from where I sat in the shade, drank coffee, and ate an apple and a good sandwich. The river ran whitewater just below; the sky was blue above. The mountains were blue-black in the distance, while the rock cliffs were red and rough and precipitous as they narrowed the canyon close around me. The cottonwoods and sycamores along the stream were just starting to turn. After multiple looks at planes flying into buildings and poor doomed souls bailing out of the 86th floor, this was a scene that could clear your head and make you think, for a time at least, that there were outposts where madness did not reach. It was the day of fishing I needed, it seemed, and what's more I hadn't seen anyone all day. Someone with a more easygoing philosophy than mine might have been content to say: "It's enough just being here." But I wanted to hang one.

Planning is important in fishing, but so is creativity in case your plan doesn't work out. It occurred to me over lunch that on this river on this day I wasn't going to catch a bass on an artificial fly. But I might catch some kind of fish on a real one. Along with the fly box in my vest, I carry a mini tackle box with a few hooks, swivels, and split shot. I don't generally carry any bait because I know I can always catch some. For bait you need a small, fine-mesh net. Mine is sized about right to net a foot-long fish, but I rarely use it for that. I have a long handle on it so it also makes a good walking stick, especially for crossing streams. And it's deadly when you need to hunt some "real flies."

I started turning over rocks in a riffle, holding the net just downstream. I hadn't turned a dozen and I had three water beetles about the size of my thumbnail. I also got a crayfish and two hellgrammites. Many fly-fishers go to great lengths to tie wooly buggers with long tails that look like hellgrammites. The best of them are works of art and they do catch fish, but none so well as the real thing. I used a #6 hook. The hellgrammite I skewered was long and creepy and gruesome and mean; he wiggled on the hook and in the water a fish would smell him even if visibility was poor. An easy roll cast put him up into the tail of a chute and the current took him down into the pool. On a four-pound tippet and with no split shot he drifted without drag and disappeared down into the murk.

A hungry catfish will find a bait no matter how cloudy the water. I saw the blue-gray flash in the water as he took my "fly." I knew it was a channel cat and I knew he was big. Then I was splashing along the bank, chasing a

"I had to use a real fly to do it, but I beat the muddy waters and lay one on the plate."
Courtesy of M. H. Salmon.

wild fish downstream. If he had kept going he would have been gone 'cause I sure couldn't stop him with a four-weight rod and four-pound tippet. But he went deep in the next pool and began to circle, pumping my rod into a hoop. I felt it was just a matter of time—my four-weight rod would break if I did horse him in; my four-pound tippet would wear through on his teeth if I didn't. And I was already asking myself why I didn't tie a fresh knot, tippet to leader, when I switched to a natural fly. I opted for patience, used the drag when it was enough, back-reeled when it wasn't, somehow everything held, and fifteen minutes later I had him at my feet in the shallows. It was steep there so I couldn't beach him, and he was way too big for my net. I threw away all caution, dropped the rod, got him cradled in my hands, and heaved him up over the bank.

I took a few pictures so folks wouldn't think I lied about it all. He was a good two feet, or better, all muscled up along his length and shouldered like a linebacker. Fresh out of the water he was crowding ten pounds.

I used up the rest of my "flies" through the rest of the day. I never landed anything, but I had a few on, including a big flathead that broke the line.

Ever since a few of those people killed so many of our people, the president and others have been telling us that our world has changed. Within the realm of international relations this may be true. For those who were lost, and for those close to those who were lost, it is certainly true. For the rest of us things are really a lot the same. We know we have to shake it off and clear our heads. Holding the country together means holding yourself together, then you get on with it. For my part, I went fishing in a wild river where I wouldn't see anyone all day. And I caught a lunker catfish on a fly rod. I'm inclined to let the trophies go, but, atypically, I packed this one out for a fish fry back home. Catch and release has its limits. I had to use a real fly to do it, but I beat the muddy water and lay one on the plate, enough for the whole family. Considering the state of the world, I figured we needed the nourishment.

Going Dry

It's been apparent to me for some time that I don't fly-fish "right." My breaks from orthodoxy and propriety are myriad. I'm not the least reluctant to cast nymphs and wooly buggers through the better part of the day,

then catch some real flies—a hellgrammite, crawfish, or grasshopper—
and fish bait with a fly rod on the hike back to the truck. Live hoppers
were Hemingway's "fly" in "Big Two-Hearted River" and it didn't seem
to ruin him, either as a writer or fisherman. The Gila River drainage,
with its odd mix of game and rough fish, cold and warm waters, natives,
non-natives, and exotics, invites its own traditions. But my principal sin
as a fly-fisher is, I usually fish flies below the surface.

Fly-fishing tradition was largely formed centuries ago in Europe,
especially the United Kingdom, and this tradition was taken up and
scarcely modified in our northeastern states. By that tradition, a fly is
selected to match a specific insect hatch coming off the surface. You
cast a matching dry fly upstream and try for a dead drift to fool the
rising trout.

Sounds good to me, but when was the last time you saw an organized rise on a Gila Forest stream? It happens, but if we limited our
fishing to rising trout, us local anglers would spend most of our angling
hours simply watching the water. So, I drift nymphs and wooly buggers
and streamers of various sizes and hues and elicit feeding from trout
and other fish that, by appearances, aren't even hungry. Still, tradition
holds a certain allure to the fly-fisher, and so the other day I went fishing
having made a vow that I would only take them on the surface. For one
day at least, I was going dry.

I started off by losing seven dollars to the government. You know
how galling that can be. It's come to be that the Forest Service wants a
parking fee—three dollars a day in this case—to leave your vehicle at
certain recreation areas and trailheads leading into the wilderness. I
always forget about this, and sure enough I arrived at the trailhead with
a ten-dollar bill. There was no person or place nearby to make change. I
was left with the choice of stiffing the Forest Service (my first impulse)
and risk a ticket, or leaving ten dollars in the numbered envelope when
they only asked for three! Having paid my taxes last April, even three
dollars seems like a gouge on my right to use public land; still, I parted
with a ten-spot without much hope that my government would put the
extra seven bucks to good use.

Upstream, at the first pool, I chose a Parachute Adams. This is
simply the world's most lauded dry fly with a tuft of white hair added
to increase buoyancy and make it easier to see. Typically, there was no

hatch in progress, but this was one of the Gila's better tributaries and I could see trout holding and wavering in the pools.

I went for the upstream, dead-drift approach. I'm not practiced at this and I'm sure it showed. Yet the fish kept rising and bumping my fly. I couldn't hook them and blamed myself, thinking I lacked the reflexes to hook fish on the surface. Eventually the trout bumped it enough that my dry fly got wet and started to sink.

The usual suggestion is to periodically false cast to dry the fly. This was not possible along the confines of this tight little stream, so I let the fly sink and they bumped it under water and I still couldn't hook them. I broke for lunch. It was a pretty spot and a good sandwich, but it was eating me up that I'd overpaid the government only to prove to myself that I couldn't catch a trout on a dry fly.

After lunch I debated changing flies, maybe even giving up and going with a nymph. But it wasn't that they wouldn't hit the Adams, and when it was wet my Adams was rather like a nymph anyway. I put some floatant on the same fly and went back to the surface.

They'd been playful, but now they were hungry, and a small colorful hybrid took that floating Adams on the first pass. He hit so hard he hooked himself. I landed him, turned him loose, and after that I could hardly miss. I got most of them on the dead drift, though I'm sure many of my presentations were flawed. Often they hit it anyway. These were trout primarily of rainbow breeding, but many had a copper-yellow underbelly showing the Gila trout influence from long ago, and a few sported a throat slash. So to call them "rainbows" doesn't do them justice. And they don't raise such variegated colorations of delight in a hatchery.

At the end of each drift I would twitch the fly, or even skitter it back upstream. This too is against traditional dry fly dogma, but it often worked. I also fished some of the pools from upstream. Sometimes this was the only cast available. I'd make a roll cast down into the pool and feed some slack out, hoping for that elusive, even if momentary, dead drift. This is also nontraditional, but it worked, including on the only fish of the day that approached a foot long. Traditional or not, I was dry fly-fishing. It was fun to see the fly, see the fish attack, and watch the swirl as the fish took the fly down. In spite of myself, I must have caught twenty trout. When I finally got back to the parking lot, still

"They'd been playful, but now they were hungry, and a colorful hybrid took that floating Adams on the first pass." Courtesy of M. H. Salmon.

empty of people or cars, I felt not so bad about losing seven dollars to the Forest Service.

Things got more interesting when I got home. In my bookshop I have for sale a first edition of Leonard Wright's classic *Fishing the Dry Fly as a Living Insect—An Unorthodox Approach*. This was a revelation. Wright agrees that the upstream, dead-drift approach is best when there is a hatch underway. But he says the dead-drift approach is not the best for dry flies when fishing for reluctant trout. Then, the fish must be convinced the bug is alive. Wright does this with a twitch technique that is more sophisticated than what I employed but fulfills the same purpose, to fish the dry fly as a living insect. Wright also has a chapter on why it is sometimes best to fish the dry fly from upstream down. He explained in detail, from long experience, what I had just discovered that day by indirection. In the end it was just neat that I had learned something useful on the water, and that my knowledge was largely self-discovered, then confirmed, by the estimable Leonard Wright.

Also, since I gave the Forest Service seven dollars too much, I figure I've got two days built up when I can park at that trailhead for free. I wonder what my chances are of getting away with that?

Hooking Up: A Brief Affair with Carp

They say place makes a difference, and in places this fish is so despised it's called "sewer bass." It's certainly not a compliment, but stop and think and it's a credit to the fish that she can live where pollutants render other species belly up. And don't forget it's not the carp that pollutes the water, it's us. But catch a carp from a free-flowing stream, unpolluted and coursing through the nation's first wilderness area, and you have a different fish, for place does make a difference. She won't jump, but nothing is stronger and more enduring, and carp, especially big carp, can make the longest runs in fresh water. Consider her potential for size—the largest North American carp is larger than the largest North American muskellunge—and you see this is trophy fishing. And then catch her on a fly!

I'd caught carp on flies before, but if I say the truth, it was mostly happenstance. And I'd caught carp on bait using a fly rod, but that's not quite it either. Any carp is fun and makes you feel her power, especially on a fly rod, but I was wanting to catch a carp on an artificial fly on purpose. So I went to the river thinking I might give it a try, although the variegated Gila has other allures for the angler, and I was thinking of them too. Stringing up the rod I pictured a two-foot carp putting a flex in it, but also a bronze bass at least fifteen inches long. One called for a four-pound tippet, the other for double that. I tied on the lighter line and would regret it.

At the first pool I caught a small bass, and at a second small pool I caught another. I was now thinking bass and had a big one in mind for the next pool, which had more depth. Also, from experience, I knew it would have carp. But I stayed with my bass rig and worked the pool upstream with a Pistol Pete, letting it drift down with the slow current, then jigging it back against the flow. No bass were interested in that approach, so I thought, I'll let it go down, then bump it along the bottom as I strip it in. This will sometimes entice a bass, or a catfish or a carp, but the negative is you're apt to hang up on the bottom. And that's what happened as the fly stalled in the depths, and when I put the pressure on, the rod began to hoop. Then the hoop doubled over and the bottom started off upstream!

I could feel a great weight and knew it was a catfish or a carp and that I was in trouble with a four-weight rod and a four-pound tippet. But I've caught big fish on light line before and felt I had a chance. The fish went to the head of the pool but turned back on her own, wanting to stay in the deeper water. It was a long run of deep water downstream from there and that's where she went, in a hurry. I couldn't stop her and walked—then ran—the bank till I got to a high point away from the trees. I got up on the high point, hoping to see the fish. She had half the line out and could easily have taken me into the backing but turned on her own again when she got to the shallows at the tail of the pool. And as she turned I saw these big yellow/bronze scales. I also saw she was a lot more than two feet long.

Well, this all went on for a while. It was mostly that strong steady pull with the fish playing me more than me playing the fish, and only her reluctance to leave the pool kept us close. Every once in a while she'd make a run and spin the handle on the reel, and I'd try to keep the pressure on the fish and the slack out of the line with the palm of my hand. And always the four-weight rod throbbed in a half circle. But I knew it was the line that would go first.

And it did, jumping back out of the water to the bank where it coiled at my feet when it finally let loose. At that point you always look to see which knot broke, at the fly or at the leader. But darned if it hadn't given way right in the middle of the tippet. Maybe the fish nicked it under water. Or maybe it was nicked as it came from the factory. Either way, I was deep in gloom.

You can bet I was focused on carp now. And regret is folly, but just try to dodge it as you change—too late—to the tippet you needed when you were still attached to the fish. I was now geared up right but, as it happens, would not hook up for the rest of the day. I did catch two decent bronze bass, but in the state I was in they hardly counted. I found

"She had half the line out and could easily have taken me into the backing . . ."
Courtesy of M. H. Salmon.

carp in other pools—I could see them—but I could not entice them with
a wooly bugger placed in their line of travel, not even when I replaced
the artificial with a live hellgrammite. It seemed these big game fish
were still beyond me, except as happenstance. But back home I went
to my library for a look at *Carp on the Fly* by Barry Reynolds, Brad
Befus, and John Berryman. I was looking at cruising carp, they told me,
which seldom take, no matter how properly you place your fly. The one I
hooked, though I couldn't see her take, was undoubtedly a feeding carp.
I would need to cast to them, I read, when they are bumping the bottom,
nose down and tail up, obviously on the feed.

At the end of the day it was a long hike out of there, back to the truck
on a hot afternoon with nothing to show. Yet upon reflection at my desk,
I sat exalted. I could still feel her power, and the speed as she spun the

handles on the reel. I saw her long back and big scales and yellow belly as she turned in the sun. At that place, in that water, she was clean as a trout, and just as desirable, only twice the size. In the end, she was too much for me and got away. Yet hooking up can be great, even if the affair is brief.

Gila River Idyll

Mellow, blue-green waters, a turquoise green canoe, blue skies and red birds, cottonwoods and sycamores along the shore—such is life floating through the Gila River Lower Box. Our craft is a Coleman square-ended "Scanoe," so called because it's part skiff and part canoe. It's not the choice for serious whitewater, but traveling as we are with a five-year-old, my wife and I aren't looking for heavy water. The Gila Lower Box offers nothing above class I rapids and our Coleman has the size and stability for two adults and a kid. The run down to the next bridge, at Virden, is about twenty miles. I have heard of kayakers doing it in a day. Such people are paddlers, not river runners. We are planning three days and two nights out, enough time to savor a free ride on a blue-green current, a couple of camps near catfish holes, a hunt for Indian petroglyphs, and perhaps the sight of a certain bright red bird.

"Watch for the vermillion flycatcher," I call to the crew in the bow.

Cherie and Bud have never seen one and I tell them that I haven't seen one myself in a number of years. Years ago it seemed I always found one or more whenever I fished the lower Gila. Only the scarlet tanager rivals the intense redness of this lovely bird, and I'll feel a lot better when I see for myself that they're not gone from my favorite river.

The flow is about 400 cfs (cubic feet per second), a good spring runoff from mountain snowfields many miles away in distant sight, and 5,000 feet higher than the Gila Lower Box. We make good time, using our paddles more to steer than to push us along. It's an easy float, but still we must be alert. The worst wreck on running water comes when you get hung up midcurrent on a fence or a "sweeper" (a log or branch stretching across the river). Sure enough, in the first two hours we must pull in several times to leash-walk our canoe under fences and around fallen trees.

"There's one . . . that's a vermillion flycatcher!" I say to the crew, shocked by our good luck so soon on the water. Indeed, it's a pair of them,

"We are planning three days and two nights out, enough to savor a free ride on the blue-green current." Courtesy of M. H. Salmon.

but we watch the male on the branch as we glide underneath, the bright red—truly "vermillion"—breast and head, the black back and wings.

I'm no birder but even I can name this better-than-scarlet jewel flashing in the sun. And over the three days we will see two more pairs, plus Mexican black hawks, great blue herons, ducks (mostly mallards and mergansers), a pair of Canada geese, and a yellow and black Scott's oriole. Midafternoon we leave the rolling rangeland along the river and enter the first rock walls of the Gila Lower Box Canyon. We are now on BLM wilderness land, and we stop on a rocky shore for a snack and to gather some hellgrammites for bait. Under rocks we find a dozen of these nasty little beggars. They look like fat centipedes and they bite, but we know the trick of grabbing them behind the head and dropping them in a jar. Trout, bass, catfish—even carp—will hammer them.

There's plenty of light left as we make camp on a sand beach. Bud is soon making sand castles. Cherie has a line in by the boat. I hike downstream to a good pool I know about from past excursions. The vegetation along the river has grown up wonderfully since they confined the cows to the uplands, and I worm through the brush to the water's edge. The pool is dark green. That means it's deep, and the depth and the backwash current tells me there's got to be a catfish in there. I skewer a hellgrammite on a #4 circle hook and toss it into the flow, letting it settle naturally into the holding area. It doesn't take five minutes and I'm into a fish. He's lively and uses the current to help bend the pole, but in time I beach him, a fat channel cat about eighteen inches long.

My life is as tame and technological as yours. I'm told that, in hopes of something more lively and elemental, some men are wont to gather in groups, circle up, beat tom-toms, shout, and confess of longings to live once again in a cave. We have escaped the primitive and now we want it back. Far better, I'd say, to catch your own meat in a wilderness stream, return to your woman in camp, and hear your kid say, "Hey, Dad got one!"

That fish, though, is for breakfast, fried in cornmeal and eaten with a bunch of fresh eggs from our own chickens at home. This first night it's pork, and not from some corporate hog farm either. We grill chops from the pig we bought at the Grant County fair—no growth hormones, no antibiotics, just good meat cooked over an open fire with black beans and rice, and a background of river music and colors on the rocks from the setting sun.

Our luck would hold for two more days—days sunny and blue, the current steady, and the breezes soft and warm. We would catch five more channel cats, each about twenty inches long. Everyone got at least one, and Cherie's carp was the biggest fish of the trip. We let two of the cats go, and the carp, and carried three out for a fish fry back home.

We found an Indian sign, scratched in rock on the canyon walls. The art of the ancient ones was a good lesson in history for the boy, and I told the story as best I knew it. I made no serious mistakes with the paddle and Cherie, as usual, kept a good camp. We left no trace.

The last day we finally saw another person, a naked lady we surprised as she camped on a remote beach. Canoes don't make much noise and . . . well . . . she laughed as she hastily gathered up some cover while we rounded the bend and floated past.

She said, "You're the first people I've seen in three days!"

I said, "Same here."

Like the river that carried us, she was *au natural.*

Sometimes Skipping School Is Okay

I had promised Bud I would take him on a real campout in the wilderness. The five-day canoe trip we took in May was good but didn't count. Now it was a hiking trip he wanted, where you learn to live out of your backpack.

The summer got away from us though, and it looked like we'd have to skip school to make it work. That's because for a real campout you need at least three days. Indeed, three days is about right for that first campout—one day to pack up and hike in and set up camp; a full day at camp to lay around and explore and fish; a second night at the same camp, with a third day to hike out. A real campout, with no rush and easy to do.

We left Saturday about noon, after the soccer game. Bud said it wasn't too much to play a whole game of soccer and hike in to camp on the same day. At the trailhead the clouds looked rather ominous, but we were committed. And we had already told Bud's teacher not to expect him Monday morning at school.

Bud's pack looked tiny leaned against the pickup next to mine. But when he slung it up, it looked full-sized and fit about right for a ten-year-old kid. He carried a change of clothes and the first aid kit and his own sleeping bag and mattress pad and some of the food. I carried my own gear plus the tent, plus most of the food and all the odds and ends you stuff in at the end.

Of course we had a pack dog along. When you own seven hounds, you might as well put one of them to work. Chance carried a dog pack with all the cook gear plus his own food. I figured he had twelve pounds and Bud maybe fifteen pounds. My pack was heaviest, but with all the help I wasn't hurting any for an old man.

We started up the trail, and the stream alongside sure looked nice. I never go anywhere camping where some fishing or hunting isn't handy. The creek had a good flow yet ran so clear the deepest pools showed bottom—there was no doubt the trout would see the fly.

Bud and Chance. Courtesy of M. H. Salmon.

We hadn't been gone an hour when Bud began to discover why back-packing is popular with a certain elite while the masses will car-camp at the trailhead. That first set of hills with extra weight on your back jerks you down pretty fast. You sweat and you puff and your legs ache, especially when you're ten years old and on your first trip carrying a load.

We stopped for a water break, then another, and we weren't two hours up the trail when we looked down on a nice camp with a good big log pulled up near the fire pit and I said, "Buddy, we could quit early and camp here."

Buddy thought that was a pretty good idea. And when we got down the slope, we found the camp was close to two nice pools we could fish without getting our feet wet.

So we set up the tent and the rest of the camp and the weather held and we took a nap. Chance woke us up a little before suppertime, and Bud said, "Dad, you were going to show me about fly-fishing?"

I'm a poor choice for a fly-fishing instructor, but I was pleased to see the boy take an interest. Bud had caught bass and trout on a spinning outfit and catfish and carp on bait; this was the last step in his early education in fishing. We went down to the stream, and I told him it was too tight for false casting, but he could stand on a certain rock and be in good shape for an upstream roll cast to the head of the pool. I gave him a brief show of what I had in mind.

He did it, and did it quite well, and got a couple of hits. At the other pool he even had one on for a while. He was already getting the feel of the rod in his right hand and holding and guiding the line with his left and watching his overhead for branches when he made his cast. He was learning where to put the nymph in the current and to keep an almost-tight line and watch for a "check" in the line when he got a hit.

For supper we cooked off the stove but had a fire nonetheless, just for effect. We ate good and watched the fire till we were drifting off in the dark and crawled into the tent. There was thunder and lightning and rain in the night. Chance came into the tent, where we made room for a dog and all stayed dry till the day dawned clear in the morning. We'd yet to see or hear another camper; the masses didn't know what they were missing.

We fried up a half pound of bacon for breakfast. Wrapped in a tortilla with butter, Bud said it was the best he'd ever had. Then a fine thing happened. Bud said, "Dad, I'm going down to the pool and try some fishing." I let him go alone while I puttered around the camp, and he went down there and made his own cast and caught a trout. Then he caught two more. When your kid picks up a new mode of fishing and takes off with it of his own initiative and succeeds, well, that's something.

The fish were less cooperative for the rest of the day. But the weather went from fair to lovely, and we had a nice hike up the canyon. We saw a coatimundi. I impressed on Bud that the coatimundi is a subtropical animal more common in Mexico, while the wild trout he had just caught require cold mountain streams. I told him the Gila wilderness, with its mountain streams and connections to both the Rocky Mountains and the Sierra Madre, is one of the few places in the United States where such an experience with wildlife is possible. He'd just seen his first coatimundi and caught his first trout on a fly, and I wonder now if Dad really even needed to provide the lesson. Kids pick things up best by indirection; we were in a special place and Bud knew it. At least I made the teaching brief. We also saw a BIG RATTLESNAKE, and the butterflies were everywhere. And the next day was Monday when Bud should have been in school.

He skipped. But he learned. He learned to do the breakfast dishes. He learned how to help break down a camp and put together his own pack. He learned to help pack up the pack dog. He learned to leave no trace. He learned to toughen up and not feel the pack so much on the return hike. He learned he could catch three more trout on a fly on the way back to the truck.

I learned that as a father you don't even need to catch one fish to have a fine time camping out and fishing. Sometimes skipping school is okay.

A Legacy of Bass and Bamboo

When my father returned from World War II, he started fishing again. He had to recover from a battle wound, but family photos in black and white indicate that within a year he was back on the water, fishing rod in hand.

When I got old enough to think things through and ask questions, I would at times wonder about that wound, evidenced by the awful scar on his arm. And I would ask about his medals.

My father would tell me that he was on Iwo Jima when the land mine went off; he remembered the noise, but not much else till he woke up aboard the hospital ship offshore. Of his medals he would say little, and his war stories were like laconic anecdotes from a misspent youth.

That scar detailed so much that he would never tell. His recovery was complete, however, at least from the physical wounds of war, for when he picked up a fly rod that scarred limb put a flex in the rod that sailed the line to soft landings on distant waters. A kid just old enough to think things through and ask questions could only look and wonder.

My father was still a young man, with fears no one could see, when he passed away. He left behind his medals and his fishing rods, one of which turned up recently by a noble gesture.

I was back east when my cousin, an old fishing buddy from my own misspent youth, handed me a dented rod case. Inside, wrapped in cloth, was a bamboo fly rod, eight and a half feet, three piece, with an extra tip, a tradition with bamboo rods. My father's name was still readable, written in his own hand on the cloth. My cousin had found it tucked away amongst his own father's (my uncle's) effects, and, along with the rod, he was passing along several wooly buggers he'd tied for the occasion. For the first time I took an interest in fishing with bamboo.

Bamboo rods, I learned, are made by hand. The cane must be the best to form a rod of strength and flexibility, and the finest is grown in the Tonkin region of China. The bamboo is split, then six strips are melded together into the final form, yielding the characteristic hexagonal shape of a "cane" rod.

Though trout are the traditional game of the fly-fisher, my father's favorite fish was the smallmouth bass. The species is not native to New Mexico, but I find it wonderful that they are here now in certain remote streams of the Gila Wilderness.

Armed with bamboo, I hiked into this wild country one day and began to cast one of my cousin's wooly buggers into the better pools. Bamboo has its own rhythm and a slower casting stroke than graphite, but by noon I had caught and released a dozen bass. All these bass were less than a foot long, but I saw some larger ones, especially in one deep pool where I blundered badly.

I was standing over the pool, looking down through its easy currents, before I realized how deep it was; the water was so clear, it looked

"After the bamboo wore him down I beached him, a bronze bass sixteen inches long."
Courtesy of M. H. Salmon.

like you could touch the bottom without getting your hand wet. Then I could see several large bass. But of course they could see me too. I caught only a large chub but marked the pool down for a different approach later in the day.

Upstream, I lost a good bass when my four-pound tippet knot broke at the leader. It had been a good knot when I tied it, but it had gotten old and worn with use, and I recalled my father telling me that when you're using light line, you need to tie fresh knots to keep from breaking off a good fish. I headed back downstream, gloomy, for I had blundered again.

Back at the pool where I'd caught the chub, I approached with stealth and this time cast from a distance. The black wooly bugger sailed true, landed softly, and drifted into the pool with no drag, looking like a real hellgrammite and no fish the wiser. The take came and the bamboo came up into an arc.

The curve of the rod went deep, pulsed, and throbbed. The fish went deep, then jumped twice. After the bamboo wore him down I beached him, a bronze bass sixteen inches long.

My father fished a lot in his life, but in the end he didn't fish enough; if he had, he might still be casting that cane rod.

What's left is a son who was taught to fish wisely and to love it well, one Silver Star, two Bronze Stars, two Purple Hearts, and a legacy of bass and bamboo.

Defeated, Robbed, Restored

The San Francisco River, the Gila's largest tributary over its first two hundred miles, is, unlike the Gila, at times taken down to a trickle (or less) in its early stages. It starts its meager flow below Luna Lake, near Alpine, Arizona, and gets a bit of help from Stone Creek coming off Escudilla Mountain. It soon crosses into New Mexico and also is soon dewatered running through the farming communities of Luna and Reserve. It is thus usually nip and tuck for the flow for the first hundred miles till the "river" picks up some perennial springs in the Alma Box and the inflow of Whitewater Creek near Glenwood. At about the same place the flow turns back west and enters an awesome canyon that runs some sixty miles to its confluence with the Gila, picking up water, fish, birds, bighorn sheep, beavers, and black hawks, but no civilization and rarely any people till it reaches Clifton, Arizona, just above its merging with the Gila. Recall that James Ohio Pattie was impressed with this chasm in 1825; he marveled at the sheep, the heights and crags overlooking the river, and had his best beaver trapping there. It's all public land, part of the Gila and Apache national forests, so anyone can go there, but so remote it's sometimes called the "Lost Canyon of the Frisco." In a year with a good snowpack you can run it in a canoe.

Looking back, I can say now we were asking for it. March in this country can be nice or god-awful and the weather report for the week ahead was iffy. The flow was pushing 800 cfs, which creates a lot of hydraulics in that tight canyon, and the snowpack was such that I should have known we could afford to wait for April and have a better run. But we put in by the gauge station near Glenwood in a slight drizzle and headed for Clifton, fifty-two miles downstream.

At 800 cfs it wasn't a flow but a rush; in no time we were ten miles downstream and it had really started to rain and get cold. Then we had a wreck. I'm no whitewater king—our Coleman scanoe took a big hit and bent noticeably in the middle of the frame, and we were awash and headed for the next rapids. We got ashore with the boat. We had tied down well and hadn't lost anything, but we stood on the beach shaking from the cold as well as the shock as the rain began to turn to snow.

"We'll make camp," I said, "lay up a day or two. The sun will come back and the river will drop and we'll still make it a trip." Cherie looked like she had her doubts.

Indeed, none of this happened. It drizzled, rained, or snowed day and night and the river, if anything, was on the rise. We had a good tent, but we weren't getting anywhere.

"There's a trail out at Mule Creek," I said. "It's not on the map but I know it, and Mule Creek is maybe five miles downstream. We need to get there and be camped on river left in case this river comes a flood."

It was a fast ride to Mule Creek in the morning, but we made it without incident. We did the only thing that made sense. With the river continuing to rise, and two inches of snow on the ground, this was not a fun canoe trip; we stashed the canoe and most of the gear in a tight grove well off the river and hiked out of the Frisco Canyon. It was seven hours to a ranch house and a phone, and late that day friends came and picked us up. They handed us each a beer. There was still either snow or rain coming down, depending on the mood of the clouds.

"We'll be back in April and make this come out good yet," I said. Cherie looked like she had her doubts.

Daily, we watched the river gauge reading put out by the USGS. The river rose, then by mid-April gradually dropped to something like 200 cfs, and now it was a lot warmer too. We got a ride to the trailhead near Mule Creek and hiked down to our cache. I saw trouble right away—we was robbed!

My guess is some other river runners had come along following a bad wreck and were left in worse shape than us. They had lost stuff when they tumped over and unknowing of the trail out had taken one of the two sleeping bags, all the food, all the clothes, and the tent. They didn't

"I returned to camp disconsolate and ashamed, only to find that Cherie had caught a catfish herself, enough for supper and breakfast to boot!" Courtesy of M. H. Salmon.

take the canoe, or the fishing rods, and they'd left a few odds and ends like salt, some cooking oil, and cornmeal. We had hiked back in with a box of wheat thins, one pound of cheese, and plenty of French Market coffee. We still had nearly forty miles to go to make Clifton.

"We'll fashion a sleeping bag out of the tarp," I said. "Whoever draws the short straw gets it, but gets all the clothes too." Of course this wasn't much of a concession; we only had the clothes on our backs on account of we'd been robbed.

"That box of crackers and pound of cheese won't last long," she said.

"We'll catch plenty of catfish," I promised. Cherie looked like she had her doubts.

It was crackers and cheese and coffee for breakfast, and then we launched into the flow. At 200 cfs the Frisco was a piece of cake; a nice, swift float, some whitewater, but the hydraulics were way down and nothing to worry about. It was warm and sunny. This was going to be the float trip we wanted all along, if we could just get enough to eat. At camp that evening I said, "Get a fire going and I'll hike downstream and catch us some supper."

I fished hard for two hours. The Lost Canyon of the Frisco is a wonderful catfish run and I caught hellgrammites for bait (none better). But I couldn't even get a hit fishing some good-looking holes. It looked like cheese and crackers for supper, and we'd be out of food before we were halfway to Clifton. I returned to camp disconsolate and ashamed only to find that Cherie, who fishes only to be social, or when there is simply nothing else to do, had caught a hellgrammite of her own, put a line in the water while tending camp, and caught a channel cat that would go five pounds—enough for supper and breakfast to boot!

From then on it was plain sailing. The weather held, we swamped the canoe once but dumped out the water and laughed it off, the cheese and crackers ran out but we caught more catfish than we could ever eat or keep, and that French Market coffee became a side dish and dessert all in one. One evening we camped at the confluence of the Frisco and the Blue River. I caught a flathead catfish there that was just under thirty inches long; I put her on a stringer, took a hike, and thought of how the view up the Blue from the Frisco was little changed from what James Ohio Pattie had seen in 1825. Of course the mountain man lacked the benefit of thirty-inch catfish, an introduced species, but the bighorn sheep were still there, and I reckoned that little else had evolved and considered that I had perhaps finally found the spiritual heart of the Great Southwest. We had seen no one at any portion of the trip, and I marveled that the upper Gila drainage, of which the Frisco is part, had alone in the Southwest survived the seemingly ineluctable exigencies of growth, jobs, "development," and the endlessly slick and aggrandizing schemes of my fellow man. We were on a limited cuisine, based on what we could catch, but we were self-sustained and quite happily a long way from the nearest road or dam and may it always be so along the Lost Canyon of the Frisco.

Four days in all and we showed up in Clifton to meet our shuttle. We pulled ashore and sat on rock for a time, waiting; time enough to consider that we had been defeated by the river, robbed by our fellow man, then restored by the bounty from the same run of water. Our shuttle arrived and we took a couple of those big, wild catfish home. Winding down from the whole thing, I was dressing them out while Cherie was putting away the gear in the shed behind the house.

"That's all right," she said, "but put those filets in the freezer. It's going to be a while before I'm ready for another meal of catfish and coffee."

Oh for a Woman Who Would Fish!

Mostly, I fish alone. Always have. Male companions tend to get into an undercurrent of competition ("I've caught more fish today than him; I'm not going to mention it but he knows it's true") that is unpleasant. Fishing with women, that tension is not there. But women who fish are hard to find. They'll go along early in a relationship, for the sake of the relationship, and may even dabble a line in the water; but even with a nice catch or two, they're not truly involved. At least that's been my experience. For the most part, anyway.

I did think I had a catch one time years ago down along the Nueces River of south Texas. This was a very pretty girl and our outing to a remote, slow, muddy-water portion of this river—an ambience right out of the deep South—seemed to intrigue her. And, later, when her bobber suddenly went out of sight, she came alive just like me. I set the hook and handed her the rod. She took it eagerly and began to crank . . . until the rather sizeable catfish on the other end put the spool in reverse, spun the handles on the reel, and barked her knuckles good. "Oh this fish!" she said with significant disgust and handed the rod back to me.

"Oh this fish"—indeed! This was a wonderful fish that turned out to be a blue catfish and battled me all the way to the mud flat where I finally beached it.

"It's ugly," she said, nursing her knuckles. "Throw it back."

I released the fish and any hopes for the girl at about the same time.

And then there was a time down along a remote canyon of the Gila watershed, the San Francisco River. It was late summer—warm, almost hot. Pearly clouds roamed the sky and cast moving shadows on towering cliffs that were a glimmering, igneous red whenever the shadows left them open to the sun. Below the cliffs the river was a shimmering green and lucid as a trout stream, though much too warm for those fish; it wound around through a riparian garden of cottonwoods, white-skinned sycamores, tenuous seep willows, and stout Emory oaks. The flow offered everything a game fish needs—slack water and riffles, swift chutes, and rapids that paced up the flow and rolled whitewater and oxygen down into the deep wash-out pools. Yet it was a river in name only; pick your spots and you could walk across it without getting your wallet wet; and how did it ever make a chasm that I scanned, in places, 1,500 feet up to the canyon rim?

My companion was up ahead at the first crossing, fording the stream and giving every indication she could walk me into the ground. Yes, another pretty girl. Woman, actually, and entirely competent in the out of doors. Tennies worn without socks revealed slim and brown and athletic ankles and legs, and she wore this pair of flimsy running shorts that, when she came out of the flow on the other side wet near to the waist, appeared to disappear. Aside from those flimsy shorts, the only other covering was one of those skimpy, bare midriff shirts so many women wear in the hot weather. They say they wear them because there is nothing so comfortable on a warm summer day, and who can doubt it? Yet they've got to know of the shock waves and savory images conjured up in the bargain.

Down river maybe five miles, we hiked the beaches, navigated the riparian growth, and crossed the stream beyond any tracks that would indicate other people sharing our river. We dropped our packs and rigged up and began to fish. We'd packed in water dogs and night crawlers. We used the worms to start, wanting to save the waterdogs for the night when the big cats hunt. We did fairly well, each catching several channel cats, and she caught a bigger one than I. Indeed he was a beauty, pushing ten pounds, all muscled up and built like a tugboat. She'd battled him to the beach on light tackle and landed him alone. When I called for a photo, she hefted that cat like Davy Crockett showing off his best bear. I was really happy for her.

Toward evening we set up a camp by a good pool, and I cleaned and filleted a couple of the smaller channel cats. She said, "Show me how you do that." I did and I knew from then on she could clean her own fish, and probably do a neater job than I. We let the filets crisp over the fire and ate them with our fingers off the grill; meanwhile I told her what

"She hefted that catfish like Davy Crockett showing off his best bear."
Courtesy of M. H. Salmon.

I knew about the flathead catfish, how they get big, and predatory, and how they are uncommonly caught in the Gila or San Francisco rivers and best sought at night. Later, she listened intently, and she wanted one too. She tossed a big worm into the downside of the pool, right where the pool funneled into a chute. I threw a waterdog right into the pool where it was captured and held perfectly by a backwash.

An hour later it was dark and a faint squeaky sound told us we had some line going out. I said, "That's yours," but she was already reaching for her rod. She tightened the drag and then struck. The rod hooped, then slacked, and she began to reel in. "It must have pulled out," she said, and I put a flashlight beam on the water where the line was approaching the shore. A big flathead catfish glared back at the beam; he whirled and ran and threw water in the air; the rod tip came down and the reel screeched. Then the line popped.

Ah well! Every angler at times is left with the same disappointment and shame; tricked by a fish, a mistake is made that leaves one with empty hands and a stifling gloom. Nor did I need to tell her that we might fish the whole night, or several nights, and not get such a chance again. I did mention, unnecessarily, that she'd set the drag too tight. And then, you explain it, we heard that squeaky sound again and, by golly, the line on my reel was going out. I picked up the rod and struck, hard. And the line, unfettered by the loose drag I'd neglected to tighten, came off in a roll and collected into an awesome backlash, a regular rat's nest, right in front of the spool. The reel was now useless and I did not deserve to be still hooked to this fish. But I was and I began to play the line like I was wielding a fly rod. And after a few runs through this pool this fish took off upstream, up into the rapids, and we followed along the shore. She offered encouragement and said "Wow!" to the size of the fish she held in the light as I fed the line in and out through my fingers. It took a strong, noble fish to run that rapids upstream, but it took the sap out of him too, and I was able to turn him back to the pool and eventually work him to the bank. She put the light on him again, and he lay there grunting on the beach, all whiskery and glisteny, and she said, "Heh, there's another line hanging out of his mouth." I propped his mouth open and he was hooked twice—the waterdog and the worm were still on the hooks. You could have put your fist in there. She was really happy for both of us.

Two big ones, hers and mine, both born and raised in a wild river, were packed out the next morning, their captors weighted down, swollen with pride, happy, and knowingly blessed with a bit of fisherman's luck. Memorable moments, but of course it takes more than fishing to form a relationship. We remained friends as over time we each ended up otherwise involved.

My current storm and strife, a far better female than I deserve, knows fishing, as evidenced from other stories herein. But as our son has gotten old enough, she has increasingly relied on him to accompany me, letting her off the hook, so to speak, from angling and camping. "No, you two go," she says. Last year I don't believe she even bought a license. And it's been several years since she's cared to camp out—a tent, sleeping bag, and all that. It works out. There is no undercurrent of male competition with your own kid; I'm happy for every catch the not-so-little-guy makes.

But sometimes I recall a foxy angler who caught her own trophy channel cat and displayed the fish like Davy Crockett hoisting his biggest bear. There aren't many like that out there. Oh for a woman who would fish!

A Question of Fish and Birds

Someone commented at a lecture at a recent Gila River Festival that there are more bird watchers in America than hunters and fishermen combined. Any of these statistical summaries can be suspect, but since this speaker was not apparently attempting any political point against the consumptive outdoor pursuits, I'd be willing to say he may well be right. Or close to it.

I read that hunter numbers are down to about 15 million, with fishers at anywhere from 35 million to 50 million participants. Some say the number of anglers is declining too. And all this in the face of an overall national population increase of about 3 million per year.

I'd guess that the fisher numbers are so variable because lots of kids fish but don't get licenses and so are hard to count. And lots of saltwater fishing doesn't require a license, so the U.S. Fish and Wildlife Service (or whoever gathers the numbers) can be imprecise or variable in their estimates.

Against these numbers the speaker said there are "about 55 million bird watchers in the U.S.A." Since no form of bird-watching I know of requires a license, I'm not sure how they get that estimate, but it's a modern era with computers and spreadsheets and "extrapolations" and other things I don't understand, so I'm not going to argue.

I will say that at the Gila River Festival all the bird-watching tours were well attended, while the only fishing outing, offered by me, was attended only by myself and my son. Others came along with us, but it was for the hike and the discussion of river ecology and watershed health and the birds; Bud and I were the only ones with rod and reel.

None of this bothers me: I see fishing as having a future and bird-watching as having an even bigger future, and no conflict between the two. Indeed, there is a certain benefit to having a hand in both sports.

Fish need water and so do birds, and while birds are sometimes found far from water, the better concentrations are found along permanently flowing streams. One of the best days I ever had fishing involved birds. In the Gila country I'll take any fish that takes my fly or bait and puts up a struggle; my favorite species is the one I just caught. With birds I'm a lot fussier. I see dozens of birds every time I go fishing but only take note of a few.

Great blue herons always get me for their size and grace; it's "great" to watch one catch a fish with a darting thrust too quick for the eye, then lift off with its prize secured in the midst of such an easy reliance on air. And the Mexican black hawk is notable. They too have size, and they are coal-black predators with a white stripe across the base of the tail. Their yellow legs are unusually long for a raptor, their four-foot wingspan almost as broad as it is wide. I have seen them flying off with fish, crawfish, water snakes, and bullfrogs so big you wonder how they got them off the ground. I like them because like me they are fishers, and predators, and they seem to symbolize our rare southwestern rivers. But there are two others that will really have me talking about them when I get home.

The time I remember didn't offer me any special anticipation of bird-watching. I geared up with the usual four-weight fly rod—I don't recall what fly I used—and headed upstream to fish. I hiked for an hour, started fishing, and from the start was catching small bass—seven to ten inches. Not bad, but I was pleased rather than thrilled.

Even a dolt like me, hardly a bird watcher, can spot and name a vermillion flycatcher.
Courtesy of Robert Shantz.

I got to a certain pool that had been a honey hole in the past. I worked
it pretty hard and got nothing larger than all those ones along the way
that I'd been letting go. I'd just decided to quit—not for the day, but to
go on up to a piece of shade to have lunch—when I saw the bird. Even a
dolt like me, who doesn't count himself amongst those 55 million named
"bird watchers," can spot a vermillion flycatcher. Vermillion is a special
color, especially in sunlight out along a wilderness stream. Juxtaposed
with the bird's coal black head, well, for several seconds that little flycatcher made me forget all about fishing. His crimson was so brilliant it
was like he was illuminated from within. Then he was gone.

I found a log in the shade to sit on to eat my sandwich and drink
some lemonade. That bird was still very much with me and I recalled a
vignette from Aldo Leopold's *Round River*:

> I reined up, not sure whether the old cow was dead, or just
> dying. She had come down out of the drought-stricken hills
> to drink, I guess. And now she lay there quite still, on the
> sandbar. A swarm of brilliant green flies buzzed about her

head, and plagued her mouth and eyes. She had craned her neck—the mark was there in the sand—as if for one last look up into the cruel cliffs of Blue River.

I was reflecting on this—especially the ghoulish flies— when it happened. A flash of vermillion—a soft bubbling warble—and a little red bird hovered over the old cow's head, snapping up flies right and left, one after another; for each a cry of ecstasy, in very joy of living. And then with one quick crimson sweep of wing, it disappeared into the green depths of a cottonwood.

Did the old cow see the bird? No. Her dead eyes stared up into the cliffs. Her calf was somewhere up there.

For a while I looked at the old cow, and thought about the little red bird. Then I rode on down Blue River.

Of course it would be Leopold, an avid fisherman and hunter, who would pick up that the vermillion flycatcher is really a vicious little insectivore in its manner of living, and to see the cycle of life—the *round river*—in a dead cow, carrion-eating flies, and perhaps the prettiest bird along the river that gobbled them up.

Or that title could go to the Bullock's oriole. One flew from across the stream and landed on a branch, close enough that I could have tossed him a crust of bread. The orange-yellow color of this oriole has to be seen to be believed, but I was close enough to believe it, and again this bird's primary colors are made the more vivid set off by black feathers in just the right places. For those several seconds that bird made me forget all about my lunch. Then he was gone. There is of course no good reason—or none that man can define—for that flycatcher or that oriole to carry such colors around. Unless we count beauty as a good, and reason enough for belief in a higher power with an aesthetic sense.

I fished hard through the afternoon, wanting just one fish of size. I changed flies but again I can't remember to what. But the change worked and I hooked one.

This was a nice fish and he had a big pool to show his stuff. He soon jumped—it was a bronze bass—and I mean he cleared the water. It was just the beginning. He would run and he would jump and he would bore deep and pump the rod. I'd like to say he was that twenty-inch smallmouth I have always wanted from the Gila, but he might have been more like eighteen; they always look bigger when they jump. It took a while but I got him to the bank. He was barely held in the lip and I easily removed the hook. I reached to hold him into the current for revival, but it wasn't necessary. He had plenty left, and the getaway when he flapped his tail left splotches of mud and river water all over my dark glasses. I didn't even see where he went. But it was back in the river where he belonged. I wasn't going to keep him anyway, and since I had touched him, well, to me it was a catch. It may only take one fish and that quickly a day of fishing is redeemed.

I don't recall anything of note on the hike back to the truck—no large or brightly colored birds, no big-leaping fish. But it had already been a day with a hatful of memories.

Did the flycatcher or the oriole, or recollection of the Leopold vignette, equal that big-leaping bass? Rare and beautiful as they were, I'd have to say no. I was elevated most highly by a big fish that jumped. Strictly speaking, I'm an angler, not a bird watcher. As such, it appears I'm a minority, possibly a fading one. But I can tell you there may be some very pleasant surprises that have nothing to do with fishing when you're out along the Gila with rod and reel.

"Allah Does Not Deduct from Life . . ."

With the war going on, and 9/11 still on everyone's mind, Middle Eastern lifeways are seldom praised in our time. Yet an old Arab proverb will always ring well with me: "Allah does not deduct from life a man's time spent fishing." Allowing for minor changes in language and syntax, and the sometime substitution of "hunting" for "fishing," it's apparent that what the British call "field sports" invite a universal brotherhood and philosophy of pleasures unique to the pursuit of game. But even with fishing there are days when you wonder if your time is well spent.

It had been weeks since I'd managed a full day on the stream, and when I finally grabbed one, I worried. Would the weather be good? Would the stream be too low in lingering drought, or high and muddy with recent monsoons? Would I be too late and find others had beat me to the best spots? Would I forget my lunch? A lot can go wrong, even on your day off.

I was up with the chickens and made sure I was not too late. Once beyond the trailhead I entered the wilderness; I would see no one all day. The stream was indeed low, but the fish would still be there, if somewhat harder to sneak up on. My sandwich was in my pack. It seemed there was no good reason not to make a day of it.

I caught a roundtail chub at the first pool. He was well over a foot long, but there is a reason this fish is not on the "game" list. Well, two reasons. One is the roundtail chub is scarce and "endangered" under New Mexico state law. The other is they strike hard but tend to flag just when you're starting to enjoy the fight. Let's just say this fish had some size and was fun while he lasted.

Then I started missing fish. I think they call it "striking short." I'd get hits and they'd be on for a shake or two, and then they'd come loose. I could see many of these fish and while some were small and could be anticipated as hard to hook, most of these looked like trout or bronze bass at least a foot long, and I couldn't keep them on either. I switched from a #6 wooly bugger to a #10 wooly bugger and watched a bass that must have been sixteen inches long come out from under a big rock and flash at my fly. He was on for two shakes, then put it back in my face, truculent, as if spitting phony flies at anglers was an evasive technique he had learned at school.

It was now near noon; I'd covered miles of stream, was drenched in sweat, and I felt half starved. But I would not quit for lunch until I had a good fish to satisfy my mind. Would I go all day hungry?

At the next run I fooled a nice rainbow. He gave it a real belt, and when he surfaced the first time I could see the fly; he was hooked good. I determined to land him, then quit and relax for lunch, read the paper, and listen to the waters gently ringing off canyon walls, my philosophy restored.

The bugger jumped and landed in a bit of slash that high water had sucked into the pool. He went under and wound the line in the branches of that slash and broke the tippet. A homily from Anglo culture goes: "The worst day fishing is better than the best day working." Or something like that. I was beginning to wonder.

It was midafternoon before I got something to eat. At a long, deep run I cast upstream and used a split shot to bounce that wooly bugger along the bottom. I got a very tentative take, but hooked him anyway

"Enough of this and I could live forever." Courtesy of Jan Haley.

and felt good weight. He was all over the pool, stayed deep, and kept going and going. Turned out to be a Sonora sucker rather than the bass I expected, and would have preferred. But he was twenty inches long, had great spirit that he shared with me, and it takes a certain skill to catch a sucker fairly on a fly, i.e., not foul hooked. An underrated fish, this Sonora sucker, with all the perseverance the chub so easily gives away. I now had reason enough to quit for lunch, read the paper, and listen for a time to a free flow gently ringing off canyon walls.

The reprieve was short. The shade was now on the other side of the canyon, and I was miles from the truck. I started on the return hike, fishing here and there. No longer were they all striking short, though most were small fish. At the pool where the big bass spit back my fly I figured this time to fool that big bass. I cast from a distance, kept most of the slack out of the line, and the cross-current took the fly right by that big rock. He made a wake in his attack and struck so hard he snapped the fly off. Well, I'd had that fly on for half the day, had hooked and landed several bass and trout and a big sucker, and been hung up several times and worked the fly free, all on the same knot. It was my own foolish fault; even good knots fail over time.

Things nearly got a whole lot worse. I sat on the end of a hollow log, got out a new wooly bugger, and began a new knot. Then I heard a familiar buzzing underneath my seat and came up off that log like my pants were on fire. He could have hit me right in the back of the calf; it was certainly nice of him to give me a warning instead. I wasn't fixing to kill any fish today, and I wasn't going to kill any indulgent snakes, even one with a rattle on his tail.

Time was running out. Black clouds began to arrive, seemingly from all directions, perhaps because this stretch of the Gila can't ever go a hundred yards in a straight line. In the last of the sun I made a proper cast, hooked and landed a sixteen-inch fish, thick, muscular, and athletic, that jumped, then glistened all the colors of the rainbow when he lay finally in the shallows, defeated.

Released, the trout soon revived in the current. I revived in the rain on the hike back to the truck, knowing the Arabs had it all figured out, oh so long ago. Enough of this and I could live forever.

"Perhaps this most unlikely place for water will be the last to give it up."
Courtesy of Jan Haley.

EIGHT

Water "Development"

IN RECOUNTING HIS CAREER WITH THE FOREST SERVICE, AND ENTHUSIASM for wilderness, I have noted Aldo Leopold's comments on just how rapidly wilderness can be lost. He recalls arriving in the Southwest in 1909 when there were six primitive areas of at least half a million acres deserving of wilderness protection. By 1920 five of these had already been lost to development—roads, railroads, power lines, dams, mines, commercial logging, mechanized/industrialized tourism (the motor car was rapidly taking the day)—the sole exception being wilderness number six, "the headwaters of the Gila River." It may be coincidence, but it is certainly ironic that regarding New Mexico's *six* main stem rivers—the Rio Grande, Pecos, Canadian, Chama, San Juan, and Gila—five have long since lost their wilderness or "wild" status, having been diverted, channelized, dewatered, and dammed up (often multiple times), starting with the Rio Grande's Elephant Butte Reservoir in 1912. Yet the Gila still flows essentially free in New Mexico (its first 150-plus miles) and for some sixty miles in Arizona before dams and diversions turn it into an intermittent flow largely controlled by man. Ten or twelve miles past its convergence with the San Francisco, near Bonita Creek, the City of Safford has installed a diversion system with pumping station—not unlike that planned for the Gila in New Mexico. It has depleted riparian habitats and related wildlife and recreation for a mile or better upstream and down. From that point the Gila can no longer be called a natural river.

How has the upper Gila continued to flow free for all these years through all those superb potential dam sites back up in the canyon lands of New Mexico? Well, from Mimbres artists through mountain warriors, mountain men, and harbingers of conservation, this unlikely place for water has always produced anomalies, the continued free flow of its principal river, the Gila, being perhaps the most notable improbability of them all. The upper Gila is still a natural river, not only an anomaly, but something of a virgin among southwestern waterways. But it's not as if nobody has ever made a pass at her.

I have seen visions of dam building and reservoirs on the Gila in New Mexico as depicted in Silver City newspapers dating back to the 1930s. But the political mechanism to get the job done came in 1968 with the Congressional multibillion-dollar Central Arizona Project (CAP). Conceived by boosters in the greater Phoenix area, and including such stalwart politicians and conservationists as Rep. Morris Udall and Senator Barry Goldwater, it was designed to divert millions of acre feet (af) of lower Colorado River water (they had already effectively dried up in that region the Gila, Salt, and Verde rivers) into canals to make central Arizona, from Phoenix to Tucson, "really boom." The logic of packing some 5 million people—the current population—into perhaps the three hottest, driest counties in the fifty states (Pima, Pinal, and Maricopa) was lost in the lust for growth. It was a federal project involving, for the most part, federal money, and it's worth asking how they ever got enough of the Congress that resided elsewhere to go along with the funding?

I can't answer that other than to make allusion to the old paradigm of western states water management. Unlike back east, where "riparian rights" gave a communal base to water ownership and management, out west the prior appropriation doctrine took hold; i.e., a water right was a property right and first in time, first in right. In other words, a senior water rights holder—the first claimant—could do whatever he wanted with his allotted acre feet. Further, there would be *no beneficial use without consumptive use.* Water in the stream—instream flows—had no value; it must be diverted and consumed or the right would be lost. It made sense for a time in settling the West—that's how the West was won—but by mid-twentieth century the doctrine had done its work and the West was a populated region. The boomers still had the political grip, however, including the state engineer of New Mexico, Steve Reynolds, powerful, already legendary, and extremely competent, sitting in his office in Santa Fe in 1968 and telling Goldwater et al. that there would be no New Mexico support for Arizona's $4 billion water booster project without a "New Mexico Unit" of the CAP. When accused of "blackmail" by the Arizona congressional delegation, he replied, "*Extortion* would be the more accurate term."

The result: in return for New Mexico's support of the CAP, the state was granted 18,000 acre feet of the yearly flow of the Gila River (about 20 percent of the yearly average) for diversion and consumption for the southwestern counties of Catron, Grant, Luna, and Hidalgo. In truth, the water was largely destined for Silver City in Grant County, the only urban area within range of the river, a town of about ten thousand people thirty miles away and across the Continental Divide in the Mimbres Basin. New Mexico's last free flow seemed destined for a dam.

The first attempt was the Hooker Dam, to be engineered at a site between Turkey Creek and Mogollon Creek, right where I went fishing and caught those bass referred to in the Introduction. While the dam site was outside the Wilderness boundary, the project would have back up a reservoir some twenty miles into the Gila Wilderness. It was now the 1970s; a new era of environmental awareness was upon the land and a reservoir in the nation's first Wilderness area could not be created, not even by Steve Reynolds.

The Conner Dam site, twenty miles downstream in the Middle Box Canyon, became the preferred alternative of the local boosters, the state engineer, and the Bureau of Reclamation (BOR). It looked strong for a time in the mid-1980s. Little by little, however, New Mexico's last unregulated flow was becoming a "cause" within the state's environmental community. At a public hearing in Silver City the conservationists outnumbered the boosters and federal enthusiasm for the Conner proposal began to wane. The U.S. Fish and Wildlife Service and New Mexico Department of Game and Fish were even less cooperative. They opined that the riparian habitats to be drowned out by the dam were of the highest category and "could not be mitigated." And they documented two rare local minnows in that river reach, the spikedace and loach minnow, proposed them as "threatened" under the Endangered Species Act (ESA), and they were soon protected by federal law. By the

late 1980s the idea of a mainstream dam on the Gila was abandoned by
the Feds. Subsequently, a brief look at a diversion system with offstream
storage in Mangas Creek was considered. It did not get far. It *might*
have dodged the ESA problem, but public opposition was still strong,
the cost/benefit analysis, fairly done by the BOR, was negative, *very significant* aquifer storage in the Silver City area was made public (making
new water from the distant Gila seem extravagant and superfluous), and
there was the matter of the locals having to contract to pay their share of
the total costs, which exceeded $100 million. When the mayor of Silver
City, himself an engineer, got a look at the cost of the water per acre foot,
he wisely declined the contract. Certain people can't see any rationale
in a stream flow beyond diversion and consumption. Instream flows, as
stated earlier, which benefit fish, wildlife, and recreation values, are not
a "beneficial use," according the *old* paradigm of western water management. Yet a *new* paradigm of western water management was now
making itself heard: instream flows do have values, economic as well
as aesthetic, and sometimes birds and fish and river running pay off
better than one more banal subdivision. In the space of a decade, what
had looked like the last best hope of the boosters, developers, and state
engineer to dam the state's last river, had crumbled. As one of the BOR
engineers told me in a candid moment over a beer: "In truth, this project
was a dog from the start."

Well, the "dog" is back. In December 2004 President Bush signed the
Arizona Water Settlements Act, which settled Indian water rights claims
in Arizona. Just as Steve Reynolds, now gone, extorted a New Mexico
unit in 1968 as a condition of New Mexico's support for the CAP, New
Mexico's congressional delegation now got Arizona to okay another ver-
sion of the Gila unit as payback for support of Arizona's new deal with
the Indians. The settlement itself is enormous, involving over $2 billion,
and has been described as "pork wrapped in an Indian blanket." But,
thanks to the U.S. Congress and you the taxpayer, everybody dealing
got something, including New Mexico, which can count on $66 million
for the four counties of Catron, Grant, Luna, and Hidalgo "for any water
related purpose," and another $62 million "if a Gila project is built."

To date, no project has been *officially* identified by New Mexico's
Interstate Stream Commission (ISC). A mainstream dam is out; diversion
to offstream storage in a side canyon is anticipated. *Unofficially*, both the

ISC and the state engineer have spoken of a massive pumping station, and infiltration gallery, somewhere between Turkey Creek and Mangas Creek, a huge pipeline (since water could only be taken during short periods of high flows) to gravity feed downstream to a storage reservoir, possibly at Mangas Creek Canyon. It's essentially the same diversion the BOR looked at twenty years ago, only in this case the project has legs because up to $128 million has already been approved by Congress.

But it's still a dog. In congressional testimony in September 2003, New Mexico State Engineer John D'Antonio estimated a construction cost of $220 million, though he acknowledged on the record that others, including the BOR, have put the cost at $300 million or more. The spike-dace and loach minnow are still listed species and still inhabit the contested river miles. Silver City and environs, a recent hydrological study has shown, sit virtually astride an aquifer storage of 15.2 *million* acre feet to a depth of 600 feet, with a natural recharge of about 16,000 af per year. The town currently uses about 2,800 af per year. Even with projected growth there is enough aquifer storage to last for centuries. A study by EcoNorthwest Inc. in 2005 showed this Mimbres aquifer water could be developed for sixteen times *less* money per acre foot than that available under the state engineer/ISC proposal for Gila River water. Why spend sixteen times more for water thirty miles away that's not needed in the first place? This is a classic case of attempting to bring coals to Newcastle. The resolution is obvious enough.

New Mexico should take the $66 million and divide it equally among the four counties (at about $16.5 million each, wisely invested, each county could count on about $1 million per year in perpetuity). Catron County wants to restore watersheds to create more water for its San Francisco River. Fine. Grant County, where Silver City resides, would have funding to acquire additional water rights and drill new wells as needed. Luna and Hidalgo Counties, along with Catron County, use more than 80 percent of their water for irrigation agriculture. They would have the funding to convert to drip irrigation, a 30 to 50 percent savings per acre that would retain far more water yearly than the ISC's proposed Gila project would supply. This political water fight is in full swing at this writing and, caught up in bureaucracy, years will pass before we know the river's fate. Studies are underway, but the chairman of the ISC has made it clear in public statements that "we're going for the water."

In the spring of 2005 my son Bud, age ten, and I made the forty-two-mile "wilderness run" from Grapevine Campground to Mogollon Creek. New grazing restrictions have restored the riparian zone and narrowed and improved the river. And that includes the Middle Box, Lower Box, and the national riparian conservation area where the Gila meets the Frisco in Arizona. ATV use is likewise eliminated in many areas along the river, or at least better managed. Gila trout recovery has made progress and a downsizing to "threatened" has recently been authorized. This will allow for some catch and release fishing for the Gila's own unique strain of trout. Elsewhere in the cooler waters, browns, rainbows, and rainbow/Gila hybrids can still be had; and in the warmer waters, small-mouth bass, channel catfish, flathead catfish, and carp as long as your leg await the angler. Native roundtail chub and desert and Sonora sucker are sometimes taken. Flood, drought, and ash flows take their toll, but with improvements to the river, and sensible regulations, the fishing can only get better over time. The Mexican black hawk, willow flycatcher, vermillion flycatcher, and Bullock's oriole continue to draw birders to improving habitats. The return of the river otter is planned and has been approved by the State Game Commission. In sum, we have been gifted a wild river with a self-sustaining sport fishery, a number of rare endemic species, and perhaps the best birding in the Southwest, most all of it on public land. It should be an easy call but, like I said, powerful forces are going for the water, and they don't intend it for fish or birds.

I still make regular excursions to the old Hooker Damsite. Motorized access is now prohibited by the Forest Service; birds and fish may now be sought in an improbable mix of stillness and life within a de facto wilderness. The same turn against the canyon wall that made the pool that produced those bass at the beginning of this book has, in the past year, seen flows ranging from a trickle that threatened their lives and my faith, to a flood flow of 20,000 cfs that scared you just to look at it from a high hill. "The river is out of control!" some said as the waters ripped their own new course to Arizona. Well, it was out of *our* control. But nature has a plan, and unlike any other river in New Mexico, the Gila is still allowed to pulse, slack, sigh, roar, and rejuvenate itself in ways we are just beginning to understand. This is the last flow in New Mexico that can teach us what a natural river should look like; the watery source of Leopold's "perfect norm."

Decades have passed and a new millennia has come since I first got my feet wet in the Gila River. The nation adds 30 million people to its population every ten years and most of that growth, it seems, is headed this way. Central Arizona hopes to grow its human population from 5 million to 10 million in three counties by 2050; some hope those hordes spill over into our own Gila country—there is money to be made by a few in the multiplication of the many! So some recommend we should feed this growth with subsidized water projects on what remains of our flowing streams. They cloak the destruction inherent in this inflammatory "development" in the even more politic euphemism: *planning.* In contrast, conservationists write books and wax eloquent, and our natural resource agencies hold a mixed cadre of enlightened scientists who issue warnings about the loss of our last, best places, but when the Senator comes to town he has lunch with the Chamber of Commerce, not the Sierra Club, Audubon Society, or Forest Service.

In spite of my imperfections as an angler, wild game fish born and raised in the stream continue to fall to my flies and bait, most to be released for their continued life and my immediate satisfaction. And all the while I stand in waters in the midst of mountains wherein scarcely anything has changed since Geronimo put up his last defense. Considering all we've done elsewhere, since then, in ruination, I can only think: *We don't deserve this.* How can it still be here? But Geronimo left a legacy of resistance; the Mimbres a legacy of art; the mountain men a legacy of adventure and the spirit of the western myth; Leopold a land ethic sprouting a legacy of conservation relevant well beyond wilderness and wild rivers. All were inspired by a free flow, a wild river, the headwaters of the Gila that continue to stand alone. The anomaly survives; the mysteries astound; the irony compounds. *¡El Gila Libre!* Perhaps this most unlikely place for water will be the last to give it up.